Author : I
Editor : Rebecca w......
Designer & Illustrator : Lenè Magro Walters

Review

Rean Combrinck
Christina LaPenna
Rinette van der Westhuizen
Katlego Hlongwane

Late 2018 Edition

Print ISBN: 978-0-620-78735-2

e-Book ISBN: 978-0-620-78685-0

CONTENTS

CHAPTER 2: REIGNITING SPIRIT

CHAPTER 3: CONCLUSION

ACKNOWLEDGEMENTS

Before I speak a word, I would like to thank the Father Yahweh for providing the fire for the sacrifice and empowering me to write this book. Throughout writing, I've prayed continually that every word would be of Him and not of myself. I believe He has honoured my request, and my hope is that you test every word. All glory and honour and praise to Him; forever and ever. He is holy!

Furthermore, I would like to thank my family and close friends for their love, support, and contributions to this work, as well as the many brothers and sisters around the world who have prayed for this. I am incredibly excited for the work He has done!

I would like to especially thank my mother and father for raising me with a foundation in truth, for always supporting me despite opposition, and for being a living example of God's power.

> " And the four beasts had each of them six wings about him; and they were full of eyes within: and they rest not day and night, saying, Holy, holy, holy, Lord God Almighty, which was, and is, and is to come. And when those beasts give glory and honour and thanks to him that sat on the throne, who liveth for ever and ever, The four and twenty elders fall down before him that sat on the throne, and worship him that liveth for ever and ever, and cast their crowns before the throne, saying,Thou art worthy, O Lord, to receive glory and honour and power: for thou hast created all things, and for thy pleasure they are and were created."
> **(REVELATION 4 : 8 – 11)**

THE BLOOD PAYMENT

In the process of writing this book and contemplating how it will be released, the Father whispered, "Don't ask for money, I have paid for this by My Blood." We have freely received; we need to freely give. As far as possible, I am trusting the Father to provide the finances to give this to everyone whom He desires. This paperback accomodates a free PDF version, available from SpiritTruthBook.com.

If, after reading, you believe this to be a message from God to His Bride, offerings may be made to partner with us in spreading this message. I pray that God would use this as a tool to align the Bride with the Bridegroom.

YOU CAN PARTNER WITH US AT:
http://www.RiseOnFire.com/partner

OTHER FORMATS AVAILABLE:
- AudioBook
- E-Book
- PDF
Purchase at: http://www.SpiritTruthBook.com

CONTACT THE AUTHOR:
PD van der Westhuizen
Email: pd@riseonfire.com
Website: www.riseonfire.com

SOCIAL MEDIA:
YouTube Channel: http://www.youtube.com/riseonfire/
Facebook: http://www.facebook.com/riseonfire/

PREFACE

Today, we are seeing the final implementation of Satan's main end-time plan. The execution of this plan has been in the works from the beginning. Satan seeks to create a divide of two groups in the Body of Christ, leaving both groups of this divide deceived. This divide occurred due to a lack of knowledge and application surrounding the fullness of Spirit & Truth, a treasure unearthed by the Father for these last days.

Those who do not fall by this deception are classified in Scripture as the remnant—those who follow "the narrow path" that few will find—also known as the Bride of Christ. The deception is also known as the great falling away (2 Thessalonians 2:3). It's not what most people have theorized, and it's already here.

The commission given to me by God has been to bring you the truth regarding this deception. This book aims to help you to understand the depth of this deception by explaining these two groups and the lies the enemy is feeding them. I believe that most of my believing readers (both mature and brand new) will be able to benefit from this revelation, because the Word of God says that "few" will find the path that leads to eternal life (Matthew 7:14). It also says that the coming deception will be able to deceive even the elect (Mark 13:22).

In addition to uncovering this deception, we will explore what it truly means to worship the Father in both Spirit and Truth (John 4:23), a concept misunderstood by the mainstream church. God is placing a great responsibility on the last generation to represent and walk in the fullness of Christ against the forces of darkness that continue to surround us.

Father God,

I pray that whoever reads this book would be blessed! I pray that this will answer the yearning in their heart to know & understand you on a deeper level. May you Lord be glorified through the reading of this book! Holy Spirit, touch the hearts of all who read this book! In Jesus's name,
(Yeshua's)
Amen

Love you
Brother or
    Sister in Christ

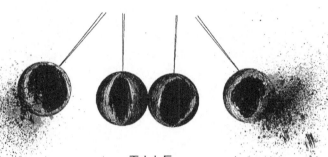

THE
SPIRIT-TRUTH
PENDULUM

Introduction
The Spirit-Truth
Pendulum

Since Jesus (Yeshua in Hebrew) ascended, an ever-growing divide started as believers swayed from the one belief in Messiah (also known as Christ). Today we have thousands of denominations, each having their own understanding of sin, Yeshua, and the Spirit of God.

From the foundation of the world, the two elements of Spirit (Genesis 1:2) and Truth (John 1:1) were there. These two essential elements form a pendulum of belief, with Truth on one side and Spirit on the other. Yeshua walked in the fullness of Spirit and Truth—in perfect balance and unity. He balanced the scale and then declared, "Now, walk as I walk" (1 John 2:6), providing the perfect example for us to imitate. I believe Adam and Eve also initially walked in this "perfect balance" due to their close garden relationship with the Father. Satan's deception led them to question who they were, which caused them to take their eyes off the Father, tipping the Spirit and Truth scale to one side or the other.

This same deception is prevalent in most of our Christian denominations today, forming two extremes important to understand. I need the stress that the following explanations are 'extremes' that does not apply to everyone in its entirety. But I would like you to better understand the deceptions of the enemy and identify where you might even be slightly entangled. In the first group (which I will be referring to as the Grace Group in this book), we see a beautiful love and understanding of the Spirit of God, an enactment of His grace, the walking out of His spiritual gifts, and a display of love for one another. However, in this love and desire to be purely led by the Spirit, the scale is tipped and the truth of

His Word is not as considered or understood. We end up with a group high in love but low in discernment. The lack of knowledge of the Word distorts the definition of sin and holiness. Sin and holiness become what we "feel" the Spirit has shown us, instead of what God has already spoken from Genesis to Revelation.

In the second group (the Truth Group) is a great display of knowledge, an understanding of God's Word, sin, holiness, and a love for the mysteries of God found in His Word. However, while this group has a genuine love for God and His Word, the love for others is not always as clear. This group is often at enmity with radical workings of the Holy Spirit—signs, wonders, miracles, spiritual gifts, etc.—and, although this is not always admitted, there is an apparent lack of these wonders in the lives of the group. Because knowledge so easily puffs up (Matthew 16:6), pride often creeps in, which creates a great incompatibility with the workings of the Holy Spirit.

Along with this pride comes a hardness to correction, especially from those in the Grace Group. They don't consider any truth within the Grace Group, because the Grace Group is not as acquainted with the Word of God as they are—even though the Grace Group does have important revelation to share. Similarly, the Grace Group is not interested in learning the knowledge and truth from God's word that the Truth Group has discovered, because the Grace Group identifies a lack of love and sometimes lack of fruit from within the Truth Group.

You will see in each group that there is a hard dip to either Truth—with an extreme of legalism (salvation by works)—or to Spirit—with an extreme of hyper-grace (salvation without works). The worst of all is that these two groups usually want nothing to do with one another!

Note that, in terms of what we are talking about, both these groups are believers in God and do love Him. Both groups also have real, powerful strengths that are gifts of God given through either His Spirit or the Truth of His Word. These strengths were hard at work in the life of Yeshua and defined who He was. He was the Word (Truth) that became flesh and He was filled with the power of the Spirit of God.

Because Yeshua walked out the perfect balance of Spirit and Truth, a part of His walk was in opposition to just about everyone. The grace side of Yeshua offended the Truth Group and the truth side of Yeshua offended the Grace Group. Similarly, Yeshua promises that anyone who will imitate Him will face the same persecution (Matthew 10:22). Most Christians never face this kind of persecution because they never walk in the fullness of Christ. They simply walk out a version of Jesus that they heard about from their spiritual leaders or the world. They end up constructing a god that fits who they want Him to be instead of who the Word says He is. If we follow the same Jesus everyone else is following, we shouldn't be surprised when we don't receive the promised persecution from them.

I am reminded of a quote: "When you're on the side of the majority, you're probably on the wrong side." While this may seem like a strange idea in Christianity, we need to realise this is what He said it will be like—that only a few people will make it, and the majority will not be on the "narrow road."

The two groups also have weaknesses that paralyze their strengths to a certain degree. The Truth Group is paralyzed by not permitting the Spirit of God to work power, love, and fruit in and through them. Without this power, love, and fruit, the Truth (Word of God) they love never accomplishes what it was meant to accomplish in the first place. The Grace Group paralyzes the Spirit of God they love by their lack of Truth—for the Spirit always follows the Truth (what God has already spoken). Genesis 1:2 says the Spirit hovered over the waters until the Word of God went forth.

But oh, when we bring Spirit and Truth together in perfect harmony, it changes everything. Balancing the pendulum keeps the enemy out, and our weaknesses that paralyzed our strengths vanish. And the strengths of Spirit and Truth grow stronger than ever because they empower each other. This is how Yeshua walked.

After this takes place within you, you will truly be able to walk as He walked.

"Truly, truly, I say to you, whoever believes in me will also do the works that I do; and greater works than these will he do, because I am going to the Father." **(JOHN 14:12)**

IDENTITY
CRISIS

The issue behind the current shortcomings within the body of Christ is an identity crisis. Satan didn't attack Adam and Eve's morality, but rather their identity. Satan knew that if he could make them question who they were, their morality would follow the counterfeit identity he led them into.

Whether your crisis lies in the revelation of Truth or revelation of Spirit, it remains an identity crisis. Satan has launched an attack of two identity crises to attack Spirit and Truth. In this book, I will explore both identity crises in two sections: **Reigniting Truth**, which deals with your identity in truth—especially which truths are applicable to that identity—and **Reigniting Spirit**, which deals with the restoration of our identity as sons of God and the revelation of authority that arrives with it.

While these may seem like simple topics, the depth to be explored will challenge and encourage you.

1.

REIGNITING TRUTH

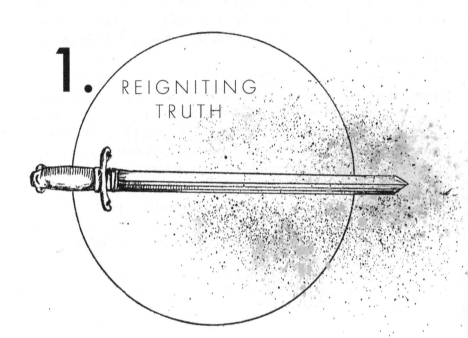

CHAPTER 1

Reigniting Truth

One day in 2009, I ran into my room and landed on my knees. "Father, I want to follow you. But there are thousands of denominations out there. Which way? If I'm going to follow you, Lord, I need the truth." I didn't realise at that moment the significance of the prayer—that it would be the defining moment that would change my life forever.

I was a mere 15 years old and still living with my parents when I prayed that prayer. One week after the prayer, we spontaneously stopped going to the Dutch Reformed Church I grew up in. I wasn't bothered too much that we left, because attending church seemed like nothing more than religious duty for just about everyone in the church. Some of my friends asked me why I don't come to church anymore. I didn't exactly know, but I soon found out this was part of God's answer to my prayer.

Shortly after leaving the church, my mother started attending smaller groups of fellowship. She would bring home revelations and teachings that were different from anything I had ever heard in church before. For the first time, the Bible was opened and studied without picking-and-choosing, we just wanted all of Yeshua no matter the cost. Surprisingly, it seemed controversial to many, but I was stirred in my Spirit that we were standing at the beginning of something 'more' than what we've been taught.

Over the next six years, God placed me in small home fellowships where we would intimately discuss scripture—testing and questioning everything I was taught in church while holding on to what was true.

Everywhere I went, from high school through my university career, I found it more and more difficult to be understood by people around me.

The Ways I studied and even walked out through Scripture were offensive to many; they made many people (even those who called themselves Christians) uncomfortable. I was confused.

I was merely taking what my Bible said seriously and trying to walk as He walked, but fellow Christians wanted nothing to do with it. The Scriptures brought me such an excitement on a weekly basis. When I attempted to share what I read, I frequently found people telling me to watch out. I was surrounded by excuses for why what I was doing was abolished and no longer applicable.

When an unbeliever comes to Christ, the natural reaction of most pastors is to direct them to the book of John. Unlike any other book, where we naturally start reading on the first page, new believers are often guided to start in the middle of the Bible instead of the beginning. After all, the beginning is "old," right? God knew this would happen, so He inspired John to write these words:

In the beginning was the Word, and the Word was with God, and the Word was God.
(JOHN 1:1, EMPHASIS ADDED)

If we are honest with ourselves, perhaps we as Christians know very little about the "abolished" Old Testament, the part of the Bible I will be referring to as the Torah (Hebrew for "instruction" and "teaching") in the coming pages.

People often find this part of the Bible offensive because they haven't paid attention to it—it's foreign to them. But why are we so divorced from these scriptures?

I grew up thinking and taught by the church that the Jews are completely deceived, and we (Christians) are perfectly right—end of story. Now, while I agree that Orthodox Jews aren't right in that they deny Jesus, we really need to ask why we seem to be so different, yet serve the same God of Abraham, Isaac, and Jacob. Where did things go wrong?

THE
DIVISION

Around 300 A.D., Constantine professed himself as a believer and the Roman Catholic church started gaining a great influence over Christianity. This was both a blessing and a curse. The blessing was that the power of the Roman empire greatly empowered the spreading of the gospel to the ends of the earth. But the curse was that, at the time, the Romans were inherently pagan. Since Christianity was exalted as a national religion for the pagan masses, it was thought that all these pagan groups needed accommodation too. The accommodation took the form of changing some of God's Torah, such as moving the Sabbath day from the seventh day (Saturday) to the first day (Sunday) to let Christians worship on the same day as the sun-god worshipers (it is no coincidence that most of pagan sun-god worship was on **Sun**days.)

Additionally, God's feast days were labelled as "Jewish" and abandoned, and other pagan feast days—such as Christmas and Easter (instead of the biblical Passover), neither of which is in the Word of God—were adopted.

This mixing with the nations is nothing new. We read it in the journey of Israel through the Exodus. God continually urges His people to be set-apart (holy), to look different from the world, to not mix with them— above all, to not worship Him in the way the pagans worship their gods:

"You shall not worship the LORD your God in that way, for every abominable thing that the LORD hates they have done for their gods, for they even burn their sons and their daughters in the fire to their gods." **(DEUTERONOMY 12:31)**

To refuse this set-apartness that God expects of His bride is rebellion against God. This initial rebellion turns into ignorance in the coming generations, and today we are born into that ignorance.

We are so far removed from God's Ways that we regard His instructions as a strange thing:

I have written to him the great things of my law, *but* they were counted as a strange thing.
(HOSEA 8:12)

Right after Yeshua ascended into heaven, the gentiles coming into the faith met together weekly and celebrated the feasts in unity. This is not shocking, since Yeshua Himself urged His disciples and followers to go listen to the Torah teachers and do whatever they say while on the seat of Moses:

Then spake Jesus to the multitude, and to his disciples, Saying, The scribes and the Pharisees sit in Moses' seat: All therefore whatsoever they bid you observe, **that observe and do**; but do not ye after their works: for they say, and do not.
(MATTHEW 23: 1-3, EMPHASIS ADDED)

For Moses of old time hath in every city them that preach him, being read in the synagogues every sabbath day.
(ACTS 15:21)

Once a teacher sat in the "seat of Moses," he was not allowed to read anything other than that which was written in the Torah and Prophets. This unity between the Jew and non-Jew was clearly upsetting and a threat to Satan's kingdom. He came to destroy this unity by introducing doctrines of demons as well as persecution to separate the two groups. The normal synagogue meetings on Sabbath, which included both Jews and non-Jews, were disrupted when the Sabbath was "changed" by the Roman church to the first day. Many Jews were forced to convert to the Roman belief and, in the coming ages, many were even killed if they refused. This caused a great divide and tension between the two groups.

Since the Jewish believers are thousands of years ahead in terms of revelation of the Torah, this has been a great issue—Christianity was left with nothing more in their understanding than what we know today as the new testament.

For many of us, not much seems wrong with that picture, but we need to understand Yeshua is the Word-made-flesh that John talked about:

And the Word was made flesh, and dwelt among us, and we beheld his glory, the glory as of the only begotten of the Father, full of grace and truth. **(JOHN 1:14)**

What Word was made flesh? No "Word" of God existed when John wrote that verse other than the Torah and Prophets. Therefore Yeshua—the Way, the Truth, and the Life—is the walking Torah (teaching). In other words, the Torah, if followed as Yeshua walked it out, is the Way that brings truth and life. This is amplified through the psalmist:

Thy righteousness is an everlasting righteousness, and thy Torah is the truth. **(PSALM 119:142)**

We also know that Yeshua, the walking teaching of God, is the Rock and foundation. (Psa 118:22). Why don't we hear this in church? Most of us grew up starting with the New Testament. We didn't build our foundation on the Rock. When we don't start with the Torah, we struggle to understanding the New Testament correctly, especially the writings of Paul (who was a scholar and very literate in the Torah). When someone who has barely read through the Torah reads Paul's writings, miscommunication is a guarantee. We cannot expect to start in the middle of the most important book in all of history and expect to understand it. The worst-case scenario is that we think we understand it when in reality we don't. This is exactly what has happened.

The enemy is still at work today just as hard as he was right after Yeshua ascended. His plan is not over, and today we are at the tipping point of that plan—the Great Falling Away. **(2 THESSALONIANS 2:1-3)**

Many are expecting some extra-terrestrial visitation or men with great signs and wonders, and that may come to pass. But I would like to submit to you that few will find the narrow path and this Great Falling Away will not be obvious or easy to discern, except by those who have built their house on the Rock:

Therefore whosoever heareth these sayings of mine, and doeth them, I will liken him unto a wise man, which built his house upon a rock. **(MATTHEW 7:24)**

So what is the Rock? We know Yeshua Himself—the walking Torah—is the Rock, but we need to understand that unless we build our house on the foundation of the front of our book ("these sayings"), our house will not stand when the storm hits.

About a year ago, a storm approached our farm here in the Karoo (South Africa), and the Father said, "PD, a storm is coming." This storm will come in my lifetime, and you will become either an observer or partaker of that storm. You will either be on the side-lines, witnessing the largest battle in history between God's and Satan's kingdoms, or you will be fighting alongside the Kingdom of God. This battle has been ongoing since Yeshua walked this earth, but has been a mere breeze in comparison to what is coming.

This book aims to equip you in walking as Yeshua walked, in both spirit and truth, to ensure your participation in that storm. For those who merely observe will not stand a chance and be swept away swiftly by every wind of demonic doctrine—doctrine that will deceive even the elect if they don't prepare.

HOW TO PREPARE

Being prepared is simple. Are you ready for the secret?

He that saith he abideth in him ought himself also so to walk, even as he walked. **(1 JOHN 2:6)**

Walk as He walked. While we can all agree that we are to "walk as He walked," because of all the false doctrine that has invaded Christianity, we don't all agree on what that means. I recently spoke to a theology graduate straight from university. He said, "Well, we are to walk as He walked, but Jesus only meant that as a spiritual statement. We don't need to walk as He walked physically." Now, whether you do or don't agree with my brother, we need to get something straight. We have been called by Yahweh, the King of the universe, to walk as Yeshua walked. He set the standard of holiness in the beginning when He started His story with man. Throughout the Torah we read how God gives instructions on what is set-apart (holy) and what is profane. He tells us what is pleasing to Him and what is an abomination to Him.

When we failed to walk in holiness, God sent Yeshua, the Word-made-flesh, who walked out God's instructions perfectly, even to the point of sacrificing Himself on the tree for all mankind—a perfect picture of the grace and kindness of God that draws us to repentance (freedom). Then He whispers, "Walk as I walked."

Was Yeshua merely being spiritual when He said that? It doesn't end there. God then sends His Spirit to come and dwell within us and tells us that He will write His Torah (teaching) on our hearts and **cause us** to walk in complete obedience to the very instructions He gave us in the beginning (Ezekiel 36:27):

Brethren, I write no new commandment unto you, but an old commandment which ye had from the beginning. The old commandment is the word which ye have heard from the beginning. **(1 JOHN 2:7)**

Today, we are going to do away with all those excuses many of you might have heard from a parent, pastor, or even those who calls themselves "prophet." If you do not walk as Yeshua walked, or have been taught a theology that excuses some of what Yeshua walked out as "only for Him," then you have grasped onto demonic doctrine designed to make you look more like the world and less like Him.

My people are destroyed for lack of knowledge; because you have rejected knowledge, I reject you from being a priest to me. And since you have forgotten the law of your God, I also will forget your children. **(HOSEA 4:6)**

Hosea talks about God's people being destroyed for a lack of knowledge, but what is this knowledge? He continues to say it is because they have rejected the law of God, and that a time will come when they will cry out, "My God, we know you!":

Israel shall cry unto me, My God, **we know thee!**
(HOSEA 8:2, EMPHASIS ADDED)

Matthew provides us God's answer and the same reason of destruction as Hosea—a lack of knowledge that leads to lawlessness:

And then will I declare to them, '**I never knew you**; depart from me, you workers of lawlessness.'
(MATTHEW 7:23, EMPHASIS ADDED)

In Matthew 7, we read about those who casted out demons, healed the sick, and even raised the dead. Now, I have been honoured to see God heal the sick through me. I have even been honoured to fight alongside Yeshua in casting out demons. At the time of writing this, though, I have yet to raise the dead. We are talking about some serious believers here with some serious faith.

Yet He will declare to them, "I never knew you, depart from me; you workers of lawlessness" (Matthew 7:23). But how could this be? We need to understand that these people were believers who loved God—at least they professed to be. But they died due to their own ignorance—destroyed for a lack of knowledge that corrupted their hearts and actions. Similarly, certain Pharisees were also convinced that they were doing the right thing in persecuting Yeshua, but their pride and ignorance of the very scriptures that prophesied about Yeshua caused their destruction.

Many teachers from the Grace Group stumble in their explanation of this scripture. Many have tried to explain that the signs and wonders performed were fabricated, since only they said to God that they have done all these miracles. I find it hard to believe these individuals will stand in front of the throne of God and have the boldness to lie to His face. God will not be mocked, and I submit to you that it will be physically impossible to lie in the presence of our mighty, perfect, and holy God.

These individuals were walking in great power, some of which maybe even by the Holy Spirit. God can use anyone. I'm sure you can recall at least a few times in your life that God used an unbeliever to minister to your heart. After all, if God used a donkey (Numbers 22:21-39), then He can certainly use anyone. God is so concerned with reaching His people and the lost that He will do so even through completely broken and sinful vessels. If He needed someone perfect to do a miracle through, His Spirit would not be able to move through any of us.

These people thought they were all right with God. They called Him "Lord, Lord," after all. Some of them were in ministry and, from the world's perspective, had committed their entire life to the works of God. Yet there was an issue: pride. They had believed a part of the very demonic doctrine responsible for the Great Falling Away: that the law of God has been abolished, fully or in part—that it is of no effect or considered a strange thing. They have chosen to be without law.

I believe pride is the root of the ability of a person to believe this doctrine. You may have heard the expressions, "The truth hurts," and "The truth will set you free." In the end of time, the Father plans to awaken His bride to the full magnitude of His Truth. This revelation bears a responsibility on our generation that the bride has not carried since the days of the first disciples:

These were more noble than those in Thessalonica, in that they received the word with all readiness of mind, and searched the scriptures daily, whether those things were so.
(ACTS 17:11)

We have always had the responsibility to separate truth from the lies, but during the implementation of this deception by Satan, it has become such a normal belief in traditional Christianity that anyone suggesting otherwise is immediately pushed aside. We no longer test everything and hold on to what is good, but we listen to our pastors and hold on to what seems right to a man. We fear to discover we have believed a lie for our entire lives; we are comfortable in our ignorance. Suddenly, everyone who attempts to present the truth becomes an adversary to our lukewarmness and comfortability. To whom much has been given, much is required. Brothers and sisters, we need to understand that today God is opening His hands to our generation to give us an incredible deposit of revelation that will empower us to walk in both Spirit and Truth, exactly like Yeshua did.

DEFINING SIN AND GOAL OF THE LAW

The Hebrew word for prepare is *panah*, which means to watch, be awake, repent, turn away and to. The way to prepare for this great end-times deception is found in the Hebrew word itself. Repentance (forgiveness followed by an action of turning away) is the key. We have all heard a call of repentance, but what do we repent from? The sad reality is that our modern culture, including modern Christianity, has completely lost the definition of sin. Sin is the opposite of truth, and truth is what sets us free. When we understand and believe in the truth—that it never changes as He never changes—then we can be set free to walk in holiness.

I was talking with a brother abroad who was recently baptized. He was concerned about his baptism because it was done by an openly homosexual priest. Stories like this should concern us. The church has lost touch with the definition of sin—the difference between what is good and what is evil is unclear. When we have no standard of holiness, we can make excuses for any sin we want to commit and say we are being "led by the Spirit."

If I were to talk with this priest, his response would probably be that the laws against homosexuality in the Torah are no longer applicable. Compromising in one area of the Torah ultimately leads to the "picking and choosing" and the compromise of all of God's instructions. I would like to submit to you that we do not need to pick and choose. The instructions of the Father are not impossible to obey, especially since He is writing them on our heart! And once we are filled with the truth of what the Bible itself says about the law, it becomes an absolute joy to keep!

For this commandment that I command you today is not too hard for you, neither is it far off.
(DEUTERONOMY 30:11, ISR)

God's Word defines sin as the transgression of the law:

Whosoever committeth sin transgresseth also the law: for sin is the transgression of the law. **(1 JOHN 3:4)**

Sin is not what we consider good or evil, holy or profane, or what "feels right." Rather, sin is what God says it is, and He has given us a beautiful grouping of scriptures to show us what is right and what is not. His house rules were written for His kids to protect them in life, to ensure that they are healthy and live in blessing. The house rules given by our Father cannot change, because that would require the definition of sin to change.

As one extreme example, if murder was sin two thousand years ago, it would still be sin today unless God chose to declare it not a sin. However, to do so would require not only God's Word but also His very nature to change. But we know that God never changes (Numbers 23:19), even if our perception of Him or His Word does. The command against murder is one example of many original instructions given in the Torah that Yeshua walked out and instructed His disciples to keep.

Now, we need to ask why we have considered some of these laws, such as murder, as still in effect and others as not.

GOAL OF THE LAW

And he said to him, "You shall love the Lord your God with all your heart and with all your soul and with all your mind. This is the great and first commandment. And a second is like it: You shall love your neighbor as yourself. On these two commandments depend all the Law and the Prophets." **(MATTHEW 22:37)**

Jesus is creating hierarchy within God's Word. Not a hierarchy of importance, but rather to help us understand God's instructions better.

2 Commandments of Love
(Love God & Love your neighbor)
+
10 Commandments
+
The Torah and The Prophets
(Further instructions on the 10 commandments)

God's two commandments of love sit on top and the Torah and Prophets hang beneath. When we talk about the Torah and Prophets, people generally divide them into two sections: (1) the 10 commandments and (2) the rest of the instructions. The general belief is that the 10 commandments are all that matter for us today. But those who hold this belief fail to understand that the rest of the Torah and Prophets describes the 10 commandments. For example, we are instructed to remember the Sabbath day (fourth commandment) and keep it holy. But how? More detail is given to us throughout the rest of the Torah and the Prophets on how to keep the Sabbath day.

Yeshua tells us that all the law and the prophets "depend" or "hang" off the first two commandments—love God and love your neighbour. He is not saying that love replaces all the Torah and the Prophets, but rather that love is the point. Love needs to be our motivation. We keep the commandments to demonstrate our love for both God (John 14:15) and others. If our obedience to God's instructions does not accomplish love, then we have missed the point completely.

Because of this, it is incredibly important to understand the meaning of love. In our society, love has come to mean everything except what it truly is. Love is associated with **feelings**, but God associates love with the **choice of sacrifice**:

Greater love has no one than this, that someone lay down his life for his friends. **(JOHN 15:13)**

Love is more than a feeling. It is an action—a choice to make a sacrifice in order to serve someone else. This is why Yeshua washed the feet of His disciples. By doing so, He sacrificed His humility and exalted others. In our love relationship with Yahweh, He made the first move by laying His life down for us. In return, He desires that we love Him back not by a mere declaration of faith, but by our actions—doing what He asked because we love Him and want to show it. Similar to a wife submitting to her husband's instruction, the Bride of Christ needs to submit to the Bridegroom's instructions. If a strange lover tried to steal away the Bride of Christ from the Bridegroom, don't you think the stranger would try to hinder the Bride's obedience first? This is exactly what we see in the Garden of Eden and throughout the ages. It has always been about obedience and choosing life!

The Bride does not follow the Husband's standard of holiness or instructions because she "needs to," but because she gets to. The difference is slight but sufficient: one is out of love from the heart, the other is out of compulsion. God doesn't want us to love Him (i.e., obey Him) under compulsion—as some kind of ticket into heaven—but because we want to and choose to. We don't keep His instructions for salvation; we keep them because of salvation. His instructions are the fruit of, not the root of, our salvation.

TRUE GRACE

For by grace are ye saved through faith; and that not of your-selves: it is the gift of God: Not of works, lest any man should boast. **(EPHESIANS 2:8-9)**

Grace is favour given to us by God even though we deserve punishment for our evil ways. Grace is not earned by what we do, but is granted to us because of our identity as children of God who profess confidence in the perfect sacrifice of Yeshua as enough to pay for our sin. The reality is, when we truly have enough faith in His sacrifice to be saved, we will be changed forever. This realization—that we deserve death but He said no—drives us to obey His Word and become more like Him. When we fall, His grace picks us up and enables obedience.

We can neither earn or demand grace. The mere fact He has given us grace is grace in itself. We don't deserve it. Too many followers of Christ have professed that they have enough faith in Him to be saved, yet de-clare that they don't need to be obedient to His instructions. If we have a profession of faith yet no works as evidence of that faith, there was never true faith to begin with! The evidence of our faith is demonstrated in our obedience to what God has spoken from the beginning. There is no "feeling" or human tradition that requires obedience.

James drives this further:
But someone will say, 'You have faith, and I have works.' Show me your faith without your works, and I will show you my faith by my works. **(JAMES 2:18)**.

If we declare we have faith, but we are not in total submission to God's instruction, we deceive ourselves. It is impossible for that faith to be real. Many Christians in the world today believe they have enough faith to be saved, yet their life looks little like the life of Yeshua. James goes on to say that we should not fool ourselves, because "even the demons believe, and they shudder" (James 2:19).

WELCOME TO THE RACE BY GRACE

Once we start speaking about obedience to the instructions of God, the question of salvation is always raised. Many Christians have been raised to believe that "we just need to get saved." Salvation is equated to the finish line. But in Scripture, salvation is only the beginning. If we live our life merely pursuing salvation, we will die in great regret.

Imagine you're in a race. The whistle blows, signaling you to run, but you never take off because you believe the starting line is the end! You can't finish the race if you don't even start it. Paul talks about this race and instructs us to run as one who receives the prize (1 Corinthians 9:24).

Similarly, the author of Hebrews tells us to move past the elementary matters and pursue true holiness (Hebrews 6:1). If all we think about is the minimum requirements needed to finish the race, we set ourselves up for failure. We need to run as one who receives first prize.

We may be quick to state that we are all running well. However, whenever confronted with an instruction of God that our denomination teaches is abolished, we often make the excuse, "Well, it's not for salvation." We end up crafting a slate of beliefs and instructions per our denominational recipe and classify those as the "essentials" of salvation.

We need to stop thinking about the "essentials" and start thinking about the Kingdom. God does not permit lukewarmness. It's all or nothing. It's about doing away with all the traditions of men that nullify or abolish the laws of God, picking up our crosses, and walking exactly as Yeshua walked. We must run the race as Yeshua did.

You cannot win a race by taking shortcuts or running over lines. You have to run with confidence and follow the rules. If you think you can run this race differently than Yeshua—the One sent by God as the perfect example—you will not win the race. But if and when you do trip and fall over a line, there is a great and merciful One whose supernatural grace heals you, picks you up from the ground, and empowers you to get up and run as if no time or distance was ever lost (1 John 2:1).

But wait, didn't Jesus run the race so we don't have to?

You may belong to the "Grace Group" if you have been taught that the instructions of God bring death, that the law is fulfilled by Yeshua, nailed to a cross and no longer applicable, or that the law of God was only for a certain people at a certain time. Let's look at these statements and let the Word speak for itself.

FULFILLING
THE LAW

One of the first statements we are reminded of in God's word when talking about the law is that it has been "fulfilled" by Christ:

Think not that I am come to destroy the law, or the prophets: I am not come to destroy, but to **fulfil**.
(MATTHEW 5:17)

The traditional teaching has been that Yeshua did not abolish or "do away" with the law, but rather obeyed it so we don't need to. Because we "can't keep it"—can't be perfect—we can now rest in that "we aren't perfect, but He is."

We need to understand that Matthew 5:17 is providing us with a contrast. Yeshua says He did not abolish, but did something else. If we are to believe that He obeyed the law so that we don't need to, then Yeshua is essentially saying, "I did not come to abolish the law, but I came to do away with it."

The law is either abolished or it's not; it cannot be half-way abolished or merely abolished in its application. The law was always meant to provide us with a definition of sin, and always will. To say it has been abolished is to say that the definition of sin has been abolished or changed. Reflecting upon history, who do you think would like to abolish the definition of sin?

Paul said that he did not know what sin is but by the law, because the law showed him what sin is:

What then shall we say? That the law is sin? By no means! Yet if it had not been for the law, I would not have known sin. For I would not have known what it is to covet if the law had not said, 'You shall not covet.' **(ROMANS 7:7)**

In the statement of Yeshua, the word *fulfil* is primarily where the deception has come through. While many believe it to mean He performed the law so we don't need to, that is far from the definition of the word.

According to the Strongs Greek [4137], fulfil is *pleroo* and means to "be full" or properly, "fill to individual capacity" and "fill to the brim."

So, Yeshua is saying, "I did not come to abolish the law, but to bring it to its fullness and fill it to its capacity." Yeshua did not take away the law or nail it to a cross, but He came to bring the law to its fullness of meaning. He did this by taking the Torah of the Father, applying it to His life, and perfectly walking it out in the way that the Father intended it to be walked out in the first place! When the Father gave us the instructions through Moses, his desire was not to burden us with a set of rules.

From the first instruction in Genesis to not eat of the tree, to the 10 commandments and the rest of the Torah, it has always been a gift from Him to us so that we may inherit the blessings of this life. His law has been designed from the beginning to show us how to walk in love and be safe. In the end, He sent the law-made-flesh to walk among us as the perfect example and said, "Walk as I walk" (1 John 2:6).

When we read on in Matthew, this definition of fulfil is confirmed:

Whosoever therefore shall break one of these least commandments, and shall teach men so, he shall be called the least in the kingdom of heaven: but whosoever shall do and teach them, the same shall be called great in the kingdom of heaven. For I say unto you, That except your righteousness shall exceed the righteousness of the scribes and Pharisees, ye shall in no case enter into the kingdom of heaven.
(MATTHEW 5:19)

He continues and confirms His previous statement of what it means to fulfil the law. He states that "not one jot or tittle will pass from the law until heaven and Earth passes away" (Matthew 5:18). Our heavenly rank after this life is also stated to be dependent on the keeping of the law. Yeshua talks about the "greatest" and "least" in heaven. This is not surprising since Paul tells us we will become judges in the heavenly realm:

Do you not know that we will judge angels? How much more the things of this life! **(1 CORINTHIANS 6:3)**

A government will not employ a judge that does not know or keep the laws of the land. Similarly, it should not surprise us that God will not appoint elders and judges in His Kingdom that do not both know and follow His law. Teaching the law, qualifies as knowing the law.

Therefore, keeping the instructions brings life and blessing and is expected by Yeshua, for anything else is the very definition of sin (1 John 3:4). If we are to walk in love, we achieve it by walking as Yeshua, and He kept the instructions of the Father that hangs off, and upholds the greatest commandment of love.

THE TREE
OF LIFE

About a year ago, while the Father was teaching me about His Spirit and Truth, I knew something was missing, but I didn't know what. I asked Him for a dream or vision as a message to His people. This unusual request was caused by a move of the Spirit of God upon me, and a month later I had an incredibly vivid vision while in worship—so vivid that it seemed almost real. I ask you to test the following.

In this vision, I was standing in a field of wheat. As I glanced down on the wheat, I was taken back by its beauty—it was as pure gold. I was amazed at how its appearance was as pure gold, yet it all moved as organically as any plant, waving gently in the wind.

Yeshua was there. He took my hand and started walking with me through this field of wheat. It was as though the wheat was intelligent—it knew of our presence and moved out of the way for us. We approached a cliff on the edge of the field. I saw something best described as a shield acting as a railing on the side of the cliff. I knew that this was the Holy Spirit. Looking down the cliff, I saw a dark and desolate place, a mountain range with lava pouring through it. As soon as I thought, *What is this?* Yeshua answered and said, "This is the Lake of Fire." While the garden I was walking through was the most beautiful place railed with gold, this Lake of Fire was supernaturally dark and without life. Yeshua looked at me with tears in His eyes, pointed to the field, and said, "PD, look around. There aren't many people here. I want to change that."

I continued walking with Yeshua and we soon approached a massive tree. This tree had large leaves and fruits that seemed bigger than my head. I have never seen these types of fruits, but the best way to describe them in earthly terms is to state that they had a similar appearance to strawberries. As I beheld the tree, I thought, *Is this the tree of the knowledge of good and evil?* But Yeshua corrected me: "No, this is the Tree of Life."

I had very little knowledge about this tree of life, as I've never studied it before. Yeshua pointed to the fruits and said, "PD, my people think works don't matter. Works do matter, and they come to grow here and make up the Garden of Heaven."

Yeshua led me away from the tree and we start walking through the garden again. I realised the great size of this place, and I saw a city that began at the edge of the garden. This city had many mansions of pure, refined gold more beautiful than any buildings I have ever seen. There were also no lower-class buildings like we see in the world, but all were magnificent. The city led up to a hill, and on the top of the hill was a castle.

I was not permitted to make out the detail of the castle. I believe the reason for this is that its glory is unseen and unspeakable. Yeshua said, "PD, I've prepared a place for my people. As you can see, it's ready. But few will dine with me." I wondered whether I am part of "the few." Then the vision ended. When I opened the Scriptures after having this somewhat bizarre experience, the Spirit took me to the last chapter of Revelation to illuminate the vision:

And he shewed me a pure river of water of life, clear as crystal, proceeding out of the throne of God and of the Lamb. In the midst of the street of it, and on either side of the river, was there the tree of life, which bare **twelve manner of fruits**, and yielded her fruit every month: and the leaves of the tree were for the healing of the nations.
(REVELATION 22:1-2, EMPHASIS ADDED)

Why does the tree of life bear 12 manners of fruits? The tree bears fruits for each of the 12 tribes of Israel. These are the fruits of God's people and, as Yeshua said, the fruits of His people come to grow in the Garden of Heaven. From Scripture, the connection between fruits and our works is clear (Jeremiah 17:10). These fruits are all connected to the intentions of our heart. We can walk out many works and do many wonderful things but have selfish intentions. On the other hand, we can do many things with the best intentions, yet still walk in lawlessness.

We yet again see the importance of Spirit and Truth. The Spirit was sent by Yeshua to guide and lead our heart. But without the Truth, we lack the discernment necessary to know when it's not the Spirit, for the Spirit will never lead us into lawlessness. Similarly, if we have the Truth without the Spirit, we may end up with heartless religious obedience without the love and other fruits the Spirit brings. The fruits of His people that make up the Garden of Heaven each month are those that form from a pure heart, guided by the Spirit as well as the Truth. These fruits and the leaves of the tree are used for the healing of the nations:

And, behold, I come quickly; and my reward is with me, to give every man **according as his work** shall be. I am Alpha and Omega, the beginning and the end, the first and the last. Blessed are they that do his commandments, that they may have right to the **tree of life**, and may enter in through the gates into the city. For without are dogs, and sorcerers, and whoremongers, and murderers, and idolaters, and whosoever loveth and maketh a lie.
(REVELATION 22:12-15, EMPHASIS ADDED)

No matter how good the intention of the heart, or how many good deeds were done in your own eyes, there is a way that seems right to a man and its end leads to destruction (Proverbs 14:12). If your actions do not demonstrate obedience according to what He has instructed, but rather rebellion towards it, you will not have an inheritance to the Tree of Life. Without the Tree of Life, you will also not be permitted to enter through the gates into His Holy City. Instead, you will be thrown into the Lake of Fire along with the rest of the lawless.

When I stood at the edge of the garden with Yeshua, glancing down the cliff unto that desolate place, there was no love. For where lawlessness (sin) is, love is not. You cannot have His Torah (Truth) without love (Spirit) or love without Torah. The appearance thereof that the world and the lukewarm parade is false, demonic, and rooted in rebellion. These are the "dogs" tossed into the Lake of Fire.

When Yeshua pointed to the field and said that there "aren't many here," he was referring to the workers of the harvest. This field of wheat represents people. Yeshua was referring to the harvest that is plentiful, with few workers (Matthew 9:37). The precious gold in this harvest is the value He has placed on His people. There is currently an incredibly large harvest of gold sitting in this world, and Yeshua is saying, "Look! There is nobody here to harvest!" Where are those who profess to follow Him? Where are the gold gatherers of this last age?

As we walked through this harvest, the wheat made way for us, and even the ground below our feet was as gold. When we enter this harvest, God will make way for us through it. The treasured, golden people He is sending us to will not hinder but will accommodate (Matthew 10:30). He will also anoint our feet with gold in this harvest. Blessed are the feet of those who bring good news!

How pleasant upon the mountains are the feet of him who brings good news, who proclaims peace, who brings good news, who proclaims deliverance, who says to Tsiyon, "Your Elohim reigns!" **(ISAIAH 52:7 ISR)**

Again, the kingdom of heaven is like unto treasure hid in a field; the which when a man hath found, he hideth, and for joy thereof goeth and selleth all that he hath, and buyeth that field. **(MATTHEW 13:44)**

In this field lies the treasures of God. Often, we think of those treasures as knowledge, but there are also treasure chests of people waiting to be opened. Today the Father calls and asks, "Do you rejoice for this treasure, as He has rejoiced over you?"

The Father sold all He had to buy the field of treasure making up the Garden of Heaven; now all He is waiting for are servants to conduct the harvest:

For who is the greater, one who reclines at table or one who serves? Is it not the one who reclines at table? But I am among you as the one who serves. "You are those who have stayed with me in my trials, and I assign to you, as my Father assigned to me, a kingdom, that you may eat and drink at my table in my kingdom and sit on thrones judging the twelve tribes of Israel. **(LUKE 22:27-30)**

The Father is speaking to a certain people who will judge the 12 tribes of Israel. Israel (God's covenant people, further discussed in the next section), represents all His people who enter the Kingdom.

These judges, however, will not be everyone. Much like our culture, where not everyone can be a judge, in God's Kingdom, not everyone will be a judge either. For if everyone were a judge, there would be no justice and everyone would do as he sees fit in his own eyes. Judges need to know the law of the land, be an example of obedience and holiness, and teach the law. God will appoint such judges for judging his people in His Kingdom and, much like in our society, these judges will be perceived as the "greatest":

Therefore whoever relaxes one of the least of these commandments and teaches others to do the same will be called least in the kingdom of heaven, but whoever does them and teaches them will be called great in the kingdom of heaven. **(MATTHEW 5:19)**

In Matthew, Yeshua speaks these words after proclaiming the instructions of His Father are not abolished. Many have taught that we will all be on the same "level" in the Kingdom to come. But this is far from what Scripture teaches. Our obedience, fruits, and servitude will determine what Yeshua gives to each on that great day (Revelation 22:12), and the greatest of these will be the judges of the Kingdom.

Yeshua continues to say that these will not only judge, but also recline with Him at table (Luke 22:30). In my vision, Yeshua said, "PD, I've prepared a place for my people. As you can see, it's ready. But few will dine with me."

Those who will dine with Him are those who know and walk out the fullness of His instructions (Truth) and spend their time in the golden fields of harvest, ordained and directed by the Holy Spirit. If we continue in passivity over this call, the enemy will come into the field and sow destructive seeds:

But while men slept, his enemy came and sowed tares among the wheat, and went his way. **(MATTHEW 13:25)**

But I have this against you, that you have abandoned the love you had at first. Remember therefore from where you have fallen; repent, and do the works you did at first. If not, I will come to you and remove your lampstand from its place, unless you repent. Yet this you have: you hate the works of the Nicolaitans, which I also hate. He who has an ear, let him hear what the Spirit says to the churches. To the one who conquers I will grant to eat of the **tree of life**, which is in the paradise of God. **(REVELATION 2:4-7, EMPHASIS ADDED)**

THE COVENANT PEOPLE
YOUR IDENTITY IN TRUTH

While we have been talking about walking just as He walked, what about the fact that Jesus was a Jew who followed "Jewish laws"? In this section, we will look at not only this question, but also why Yeshua *really* had to die. It might seem obvious at first, but God's plan of coming in the flesh had a much deeper meaning unbeknown to most—also known as "The Great Mystery." This mystery, even though in our Bibles, is one of the most incredible revelations God is revealing in this age.

When you understand this mystery, you will gain a much deeper grasp of your identity and the inheritance of truth that comes with it. God started this awakening around 2009, and it has come to be known as the "Ephraim awakening" or "the regathering" by many. This story starts in the beginning with Abraham. God came to Abraham and gave him a promise: that He will multiply Abraham's seed as many as the stars in the heavens (Genesis 17:19) because of Abraham's faith. From Abraham came Isaac, and from Isaac came Jacob. After wrestling with an angel, God changed Jacob's name to Israel (Genesis 35:10). From Jacob (Israel), the 12 sons of Israel were born. These 12 sons went forth to form the 12 tribes of Israel that Yahweh saved from Egypt and brought through the wilderness to a land flowing with milk and honey.

Throughout this journey that stretches across the first five books of Scripture, God continually warns Israel that if they depart from His Torah (teaching), He will remove Himself from their midst and their enemies will consume them. He also warns them that He will scatter them amongst the nations, out of the land He promised (Deuteronomy 4:27). On the other hand, God promises that if they are obedient, they will not have the diseases of Egypt (Deuteronomy 7:15), there will not be a barren man or women in their midst (Exodus 23:26), the rain will come in its season (Leviticus 26:4), and many more blessings. These blessings and curses are connected to whether Israel would *shema*, which is the Hebrew concept of hearing and obeying.

In most of Christianity, we have a western Greek mindset. In this cultural mindset, we can say words that bear no meaning. It is culturally acceptable to speak more than we do. The Shema Hebrew mindset (the mindset God communicates) is hearing and obeying. If you hear but you fail to obey, you fail. Hearing alone bears no fruit—there is no instruction on merely hearing. God requires us to hear and follow through with action. The modern church is full of sickness, barren men and women, and many other curses. God stated that, if we are obedient, we will not see these things. What has happened?

This issue is the same one that has caused over 33 thousand denominations within Christianity: we don't know who we are! If we knew who we were, we wouldn't have tried to figure this out over 33 thousand times. If we knew who we were, there would be unity, understanding, and peace in what we should do and where we are heading. Right now, there is chaos, because we have started to change definitions. We have failed to allow Scripture to define Scripture.

This is how the Father has given us Scripture: The first time He mentions something in the inspired Word of God, He defines it. He gives us a definition of the concept. This definition can never change or be modified, because that would require Him to change His mind about His Word (Truth). We know that Yeshua is the Word made flesh. In order for the Word to change, Yeshua needs to change too. God—eternally righteous and perfect—did not give us broken or imperfect instructions; His Word (the Truth) does not need to change or be improved upon.

For I am the LORD, I change not **(MALACHI 3:6)**

Truth will always be truth. Start changing one definition innocently, and two thousand years later that slight shift of the ship's rudder has steered you so far off course that you have no idea where you are or where you are going anymore.

This was the urgent issue that distressed me and caused me to fall on my knees for truth. *Father, I'm sick of all these denominations.* You need to show me which way.

Of course, we all believe ourselves to be in truth, but today, let's allow Scripture to define Scripture. Let us forget about what our church pastor, family, or friends taught us about Him, and let's see what He says about Himself.

This is the covenant made between God and Israel:

Keep therefore the words of this covenant, and do them, that ye may prosper in all that ye do. Ye stand this day all of you before the LORD your God; your captains of your tribes, your elders, and your officers, with all the men of Israel, Your little ones, your wives, and thy **stranger** that is in thy camp, from the hewer of thy wood unto the drawer of thy water: That thou shouldest enter into covenant with the LORD thy God, and into his oath, which the LORD thy God maketh with thee this day: That he may establish thee today for a people unto himself, and that he may be unto thee a God, as he hath said unto thee, and as he hath sworn unto thy fathers, to Abraham, to Isaac, and to Jacob. **Neither with you only** do I make this covenant and this oath; But with him that standeth here with us this day before the LORD our God, and also **with him that is not here with us this day**. **(DEUTERONOMY 29:9-15, EMPHASIS ADDED)**

As the Israelites enter the promised land, God tells them who He is making this covenant with. He first states that He is making it with the native born from the 12 tribes of Israel, but then makes an interesting statement. He says it is with the **strangers** in their midst as well. Furthermore, He ends with stating that the covenant is with not only those present there, but also with "him that is not here with us this day." But who are these people?

When God struck Egypt with the plagues, there were many Egyptians that witnessed the splendour of God and decided to fear and follow this mighty God of Israel. We read about these mixed multitudes or "strangers" who joined Israel along the journey throughout the Torah (Exodus 12:49). The bottom line is this covenant is made out not only to the native born, and not only to those present where they were given, but also to everyone who calls on the name of Yahweh and would like to follow Him—whether native or stranger—so that He can be our God, and we can be His set-apart people (Deuteronomy 29:13).

THE LOST SHEEP OF THE HOUSE OF ISRAEL

But he answered and said, I am not sent but unto the lost sheep of the house of Israel. **(MATTHEW 15:24)**

If Yeshua came only for the scattered sheep of the House of Israel, then what about the gentiles? From what we've discussed, there was already a mixed multitude within the House of Israel from Egypt. Additionally, Paul states that gentiles not of the native born become "grafted into" the olive tree (Romans 11:24). But what is this olive tree? Again, we cannot change definitions; we need to use the definition given by God Himself from the beginning:

The LORD once called you [Israel] 'a green olive tree, beautiful with good fruit.' **(JEREMIAH 11:16 ESV)**

All who came out of Egypt or joined Israel in the journey through the wilderness, who called on the God of Abraham, Isaac, and Jacob, became "grafted in" and part of the House of Israel. In Revelation, there are only 12 gates to accommodate for the 12 tribes of Israel. There is no "gentile" or "church" gate. We enter through the gate of whichever tribe we have been grafted into:

It had a great, high wall, with twelve gates, and at the gates twelve angels, and on the gates the names of the twelve tribes of the sons of Israel were inscribed. On the east three gates, on the north three gates, on the south three gates, and on the west three gates. **(REVELATION 21:12-13)**

As Israel enters the promised land, they come under various kings throughout the ages. One of which is the famous king Solomon, whose heart was drawn away to the idols of his many wives. After God warned Israel numerous times before, He split the 12 tribes into two kingdoms and scattered them amongst the pagan gentile nations (1 Kings 11:31).

The two kingdoms became known as the Northern Kingdom of Israel (10 tribes) and the Southern Kingdom of Judah (2 tribes). The two tribes in the Kingdom of Judah that broke away from the 10 were the tribe of Benjamin and the tribe of Judah. In 722 BC, the House of Israel was scattered into Assyria (Hosea 8:8), and in 586 BC, the House of Judah was scattered into Babylon. (See also: Jeremiah 50:17, Ezekiel 34:12, Amos 9:9, Ezekiel 11:16)

As a shepherd seeketh out his flock in the day that he is among his sheep that are scattered; so will I seek out my sheep, and will deliver them out of all places where they have been scattered in the cloudy and dark day. **(EZEKIEL 34:12)**

For, lo, I will command, and I will sift the house of Israel among all nations, like as corn is sifted in a sieve, yet shall not the least grain fall upon the earth. **(AMOS 9:9)**

God defines this scattered people as the "scattered sheep." Within them are not only the direct descendants of Abraham, but also the mixed multitude that joined from Egypt and throughout the ages to follow the God of Israel.

The Southern House of Judah returned from Babylon and have retained their identity to this very day; they make up the modern identity of the Jewish people. Keeping their identity was important, because the Messiah was prophesied to come through the line of Judah (John 7:42). That is why He is recognized as a Jewish Messiah even today. However, the House of Israel (10 tribes) never returned and completely lost their identity.

THE PROBLEM OF DIVORCE

The reason the 10 tribes from the House of Israel lost their identity was because God divorced the House of Israel:

And I saw, when for all the causes whereby backsliding (House of) Israel committed adultery I had put her away, and **given her a bill of divorce**; yet her treacherous sister (House of) Judah feared not, but went and played the harlot also.
(JEREMIAH 3:8, EMPHASIS ADDED)

The reason for this bill of divorce is found in Hosea:

My people are destroyed for **lack of knowledge**: because thou hast rejected knowledge, I will also reject thee, that thou shalt be no priest to me: seeing thou hast **forgotten the law** of thy God, I will also forget thy children.
(HOSEA 4:6, EMPHASIS ADDED)

While both houses went whoring amongst the nations, God gave only Israel a bill of divorce. This is a serious problem, because God's own Word states that when the wife of a husband goes to whore with another and she is divorced, she cannot return to her former husband. This means that God's own Word states that He cannot have His bride back:

Her former husband, which sent her away, may not take her again to be his wife, after that she is defiled; for that is abomination before the LORD: and thou shalt not cause the land to sin, which the LORD thy God giveth thee for an inheritance.
(DEUTERONOMY 24:4)

They say, if a man put away his wife, and she go from him, and become another man's, shall he return unto her again? shall not that land be greatly polluted? but thou hast played the harlot with many lovers; yet return again to me, saith the LORD. **(JEREMIAH 3:1)**

This is the great mystery! For centuries, and up to today, Jewish rabbis have been trying to solve how God will take His wife of whoredom back without transgressing His own Word (Hosea 2:23):

The Challenging question that arises now and that the Rabbis will have to resolve, is: How does HaShem 'remarry' the Bride whom He divorced – for this is forbidden by His Own Torah? (Rabbi Ephraim Sprecher, Commonwealth of Israel)

In Romans 7:1, Paul solves the mystery. He states that the law is binding on a person only as long as he lives, but if a partner dies, there is a release from the law. For when we are dead, we are not subject to the law anymore. This means that the only way for God to get His bride back was for Him to die! His death means that she is released from the law of marriage and can marry whomever she wishes. The Father then raised Yeshua from the dead, and He became a bachelor eligible for remarriage.

THE VOW

When Abraham sent his servant to find a bride for Isaac, the servant made a vow by placing his hand on Abraham's thigh. The side (where a sword would hang)—in Abraham's case, his thigh—represented authority and symbolised the making of a vow. When Yeshua died on the cross, the wedding vows for the covenant were made. Yeshua was struck in His side, and the blood and water of the covenant were poured out. The water represents the new creation we become through His sacrifice by being cleansed through water baptism. The baptism is the burial site for the "old man," and after dying (going into the water), we come up and are resurrected with Yeshua unto new life as a new creation. The blood poured out of His side represents the atonement of our sins.

When atonement is made by giving a life for a life as He did for us, obedience to our end of the covenant is a requirement. When the old covenant was broken by Israel, those who broke it were just as dead as the animal that made atonement for their sins, as seen in the golden calf and many other incidents, where many died in their sin.

I would like to also remind you of the incident of the quail, where the judgement of God came upon Israel's sin. Aaron and Moses ran to make an offering and, as soon as the offering touched the altar, the plague stopped (Numbers 16:47). Israel had a sacrifice, broke their end of the deal (covenant), and were declared just as dead as the animal that previously atoned for their sins.

God in the flesh never broke the covenant and was a spotless lamb slain as our new blood covenant, to restore our relationship with Him. He was struck in His side and the wedding vow was made with His blood and water pouring out. That wedding vow was the Torah, now written on our hearts:

But this shall be the covenant that I will make with the house of Israel; After those days, saith the LORD, I will put my law [Torah] in their inward parts, and write it in their hearts; and will be their God, and they shall be my people. **(JEREMIAH 31:33)**

If we are in covenant, we are required to follow the rules of the covenant—not what "feels" right. If any break the covenant, the consequence is to die just as the offering (Yeshua) died. But His resurrection means we are raised with our sacrifice unto new life. The old passes away and the new comes. This means that our resurrection in Him changes our nature from an old, pre-resurrection man into a man raised with Him. We become reborn.

With this change of nature is a natural inclination to follow God's instructions, because we are empowered by the Spirit that raised Yeshua from the dead.

Jesus answered, 'Verily, verily, I say unto thee, Except a man be born of water and of the Spirit, he cannot enter into the kingdom of God. **(JOHN 3:5)**

Breaking the covenant now in comparison to breaking the old covenant is much more serious. People believe that God isn't the same just God of the Old Testament, but He never changes. The value of our atoning sacrifice is now much higher. This means the consequence of trampling it underfoot is much worse as well.

Yeshua introduced a higher standard of holiness the letter of the law did not require. For example, instead of simply not committing the act of adultery, He requires us to not even look at a woman with lust (Matthew 5:28). He went where the law could not go, and requires obedience even from our hearts. In the old covenant, we were judged by the Torah written on stone. In the new covenant, we will be judged much more strictly—by the Torah written on our hearts.

Many may believe this to be easier, because we know our hearts. But this is a deception, for the Word states our hearts are beyond our understanding and deceitfully wicked (Jeremiah 17:9). By the law we were judged for not caring for the poor; by our hearts we are judged by our intentions when we do care for them. Did we do it to be seen by others, or because we truly love God and our neighbour? On Judgement Day, the tablets of our hearts with our intentions will be used to testify against us.

Continuing in deliberate sin after being resurrected with Him is trampling underfoot the covenant, and it upsets the Spirit of Grace. In our continuous, habitual sin, the offering of Yeshua becomes null and void without true repentance in speech and action (shema):

For if we sin wilfully after we have received the knowledge of the truth, there remaineth no more sacrifice for sins, but a certain fearful looking for of judgment and fiery indignation, which shall devour the adversaries.

He that despised Moses' law died without mercy under two or three witnesses. Of how much sorer punishment, suppose ye, shall he be thought worthy, who hath trodden underfoot the Son of God, and hath counted the blood of the covenant, wherewith he was sanctified, an unholy thing, and hath done despite unto the Spirit of grace?

For we know him that hath said, Vengeance belongeth unto me, I will recompense, saith the Lord. And again, The Lord shall judge his people. It is a fearful thing to fall into the hands of the living God. **(HEBREWS 10:26-31)**

The false hyper-grace concept introduced into western churches that renders wilful and rebellious sin after repentance "acceptable" will render the sacrifice of Yeshua null and void for many. For if we continue sinning after coming to the knowledge of the truth, "there no longer remains a sacrifice for sins."

Just as Adam's bride was created from his side, Yeshua was struck in His side, and out poured the blood and water that redeemed and restored relationship with His bride. We (the new creation in Him) were created from Yeshua's side and created from the foundation of the world for the fulfilment of God's divine purpose in Yeshua—a real illustration of His love for us.

ONE LAW

As briefly mentioned, it is important for us to remember and understand that the 12 tribes as a collective aren't the Jews as we know them today, as the Jews made up only a portion of the tribes. Therefore, we cannot call certain instructions within God's Word "Jewish" or "Christian"; there is one instruction for His people.

The definition of sin is the transgression of the law (1 John 3:4), and the law shows us what sin is (Romans 7:7). Why would God give two different definitions of sin to separate groups of His people? Is what is sin to one group not sin for another? Can the definition of evil change over time? I would like to submit that God didn't give different instructions to different people groups. But through our commandments and teachings of men, we have caused a separation not only between Jews and non-Jews, but also between 33 thousand denominations—all steering in different directions fuelled by the changing of definitions to create our own version of Jesus. The clearest factor that sets any god aside from another is the scriptures/instructions and revelation given. The instructions that you follow determine the god you serve and the walk you follow. Do you walk as Yeshua walked? For He is coming for a Bride that walks as He walked.

God does not change His mind over what He has said in the beginning.

God doesn't expect only a certain group of people to be obedient to His instructions, but rather all people who state that they follow Him.

If you read through the entire Torah, you will see a certain verse come up over 15 times:

One law shall be to him that is homeborn, and unto the stranger that sojourneth among you. **(EXODUS 12:49)**
See also: Exodus 12:19, Leviticus 16:29, Leviticus 17:15, Leviticus 18:26, Leviticus 19:34, Leviticus 24:16, Leviticus 24:22, Numbers 9:14, Numbers 15:29, Numbers 15:30; and Ezekiel 47:22 (prophecy)

In the above verses, God continually warns that everyone who would like to follow Him needs to be obedient. If you don't want to be obedient, then you cannot remain within the camp of those who follow Him. Those who were disobedient to His Torah did not enter the promised land but suffered under numerous curses that they brought upon themselves through their disobedience. You cannot be in a marriage yet continually break the marriage covenant.

One law was given for everyone. There was no Jew or gentile then, and there is no Jew or gentile today—for we all one in the God that is One. There is no "Jewish law" and "Christian/gentile law" in the scriptures, but One Law, and One Messiah who has become the walking Torah (teaching) for all to imitate.

The Torah is now written on your heart. God is changing your nature, and you have a Holy Spirit that is causing and inclining you to follow His Torah:

And I will put my spirit within you, and **cause you** to walk in my statutes, and ye shall keep my judgments, and do them. **(EZEKIEL 36:27, EMPHASIS ADDED)**

All scripture is given by inspiration of God, and is profitable for doctrine, for reproof, for correction, for instruction in righteousness. **(2 TIMOTHY 3:16)**

The only thing that will prevent your obedience is false teachings of men that go against the voice of the Spirit. If the Spirit calls you to keep the Sabbath day holy, yet men teach that the fourth commandment is abolished, you will be confused and destroyed for a lack of knowledge of the truth—the same reason the House of Israel was divorced in the first place.

It is important to note that, at the time of Ezekiel's writing above, the only "law" that existed is the same law God writes on your heart: the Torah and Prophets. Additionally, "all scripture" mentioned by Timothy refers to the Torah and Prophets as well, for there was no other "scripture" at the time of writing. In this, I am not attempting to discredit the New Testament, for I believe this statement applies from Genesis to Revelation. But I would like to make you understand what scripture Timothy was specifically referring to at the time of writing.

THE ETERNAL COVENANT

Because God is unchanging, and the definition of sin does not change, I would like to show you His eternal covenant.

Old Testament
And I will establish my covenant between me and thee and thy seed after thee in their generations for an **everlasting covenant**, to be a God unto thee, and to thy seed after thee. **(GENESIS 17:7, EMPHASIS ADDED)**

And God said, Sarah thy wife shall bear thee a son indeed; and thou shalt call his name Isaac: and I will establish my covenant with him for an **everlasting covenant**, and with his seed after him. **(GENESIS 17:19, EMPHASIS ADDED)**

And confirmed the same unto Jacob for a law, and to Israel for an **everlasting covenant**.
(PSALM 105:10, EMPHASIS ADDED)

The earth also is defiled under the inhabitants thereof; because they have transgressed the laws, changed the ordinance, broken the **everlasting** covenant.
(ISAIAH 24:5, EMPHASIS ADDED)

As previously discussed, there is one people in Him. His people started with Abraham, and through Abraham's seed all nations were blessed. Through the ages, God opened the door of relationship not only to the native-born and bloodline of Abraham, Isaac, and Jacob, but also to the "strangers" and "mixed multitudes" that saw the light native-born were carrying. Paul drives this further in Romans when he states that those who were previously gentiles now become grafted and adopted into the olive tree—that is, Israel—and all become as native-born through Jesus. Israel is and will always be the truthful identity of God's people. It's not about bloodline; it's about sonship.

The covenant given to this people is known throughout the Torah and the Prophets as the "everlasting" or "eternal" covenant. Furthermore, instructions therein are repeatedly called "everlasting statutes to be kept throughout your generations forever." (See *Numbers 15:15, Genesis 17:9, Exodus 12:14, Exodus 12:17, Exodus 31:13, Leviticus 3:17, Leviticus 23:21, Leviticus 23:31, Numbers 10:8, Numbers 15:23.*)

We know that the coming of Jesus was not a last resource, but rather the plan from the beginning. He was set apart for the calling before the foundation of the world (John 1:1). God did not give His people a covenant He calls "everlasting" only to nullify it. He made no mistake. The nullifying of the covenant would mean that God transgressed His own promise of an everlasting covenant. Interestingly, the New Testament also calls this covenant everlasting:

New Testament
Now the God of peace, that brought again from the dead our Lord Jesus, that great shepherd of the sheep, through the blood of the **everlasting covenant**.
(HEBREWS 13:20, EMPHASIS ADDED)

Ye are the children of the prophets, and of **the covenant which God made with our fathers**, saying unto Abraham, And in thy seed shall all the kindreds of the earth be blessed. **(ACTS 3:25, EMPHASIS ADDED)**

The everlasting covenant exists from everlasting to everlasting, just as His truth and essence is from everlasting to everlasting. The covenant was not abolished by God; however, it was broken by us:

For if that first covenant had been faultless, then should no place have been sought for the second. For **finding fault with them**, he saith, Behold, the days come, saith the Lord, when I will make a **new covenant** with the house of Israel and with the house of Judah: Not according to the covenant that I made with their fathers in the day when I took them by the hand to lead them out of the land of Egypt; because they **continued not in my covenant**, and I regarded them not, saith the Lord. **(HEBREWS 8:7-9, EMPHASIS ADDED)**

We read that the "fault" in the covenant was not the covenant itself, but rather the inability of the people to keep it. It was not His covenant itself that was broken, but the people—and in their brokenness, they broke the covenant. The old covenant was perfect, holy, pure, righteous—completely without fault! This is per scripture but contrary to mainstream teaching. God did not give us something broken. He gave us perfection. But perfection was given to imperfection.

Because we who are imperfect could not obey perfection, He poured out a perfect Spirit on Shavuot (Pentecost) and writes the perfect law on our heart (Hebrew 8:10), changing our nature. We now become perfect in Spirit and have no more excuse for disobedience. Our new nature now can and wants to walk out His Torah written on our heart.

The law of the LORD is perfect, converting the soul: the testimony of the LORD is sure, making wise the simple. The statutes of the LORD are right, rejoicing the heart: the commandment of the LORD is pure, enlightening the eyes. **(PSALM 19:7)**

More to be desired are they than gold, yea, than much fine gold: sweeter also than honey and the honeycomb.
(PSALM 19:10)

THE OLD, RENEWED?

Because we broke the everlasting covenant, a crisis came forth. Breaking an everlasting marriage covenant brings forth an everlasting consequence: eternal death and divorce from God. As mentioned, however, Yeshua's death released us from the law that bound us to that broken covenant, and in our resurrection with Him we can enter a new covenant with Him. This covenant can be considered both old and new in different ways—old in that the terms of the covenant have not changed (it remains to be the Torah given by God on Mount Sinai), but new in that it is now written on our "inward parts." Obedience to it brings blessing, while disobedience bears consequence.

However, this covenant is not like the old which we broke, for the administration of the covenant is new. Instead of having a mediator of man (Levitical high priest) like in the old covenant because we were afraid of God, God now gives His Son as high priest to intercede and atone. At Mount Sinai, we wanted it our way; we were afraid of God, didn't want to hear from Him directly, and rejected His Spirit. We wanted Moses to speak on our behalf. God allowed us to have our way, but 12 hundred years later He poured out His Spirit over a broken people—something He has always planned and wanted to do—enabling them to keep the everlasting marriage covenant as His Bride ought to. The Spirit convicts and changes us into a nature with the ability of keeping the everlasting covenant.

We will explore the events surrounding the giving of Spirit and Truth further in a coming section titled "Marks of Shavuot."

LEGALISM

It is important for me to explain to you that many have attempted to add or take away from the law of God. Many man-made traditions, doctrines, and laws have invaded both Christianity and Judaism. For example, many sects of Judaism have added a large amount of man-made laws (not in scripture) to their religion that ends up burdening believers to the point of legalistic observance. We observe this in how certain Pharisees persecute the disciples of Christ for not washing their hands before they eat (Matthew 15:2), a man-made traditional teaching not grounded in the scriptures. Don't get me wrong, washing your hands before you eat may be a clever idea, but not doing so is not sin, for it is not against the instruction of Father. If there is no law against something, it is not sin (Romans 4:15), for the law shows us what sin is (1 John 3:4).

Today, we are not referring to these added man-made traditions or laws surrounding how to follow God, for often they take away from God's original word and burden our walk. God never brought the Israelites out of Egyptian slavery to enslave them yet again with His law. His Torah is not slavery, but freedom, and those who keep it are blessed (James 1:25). But various religious organisations have been enslaving men with their man-made laws, as addressed by Jesus:

"... thus making void the word of God by your tradition that you have handed down. And many such things you do."
(MARK 7:13)

Legalism is a real danger, but the term is often used for the wrong purposes. Many call the idea of following the law of God legalism. But let us understand the definition.

Legalism is the belief that salvation comes from strict adherence to the law, also known as the "works-based gospel." As mentioned, we see this idea prevalent in the doctrines of some Pharisees in their persecution of Yeshua and His disciples:

But some men came down from Judea and were teaching the brothers, "Unless you are circumcised according to the custom of Moses, you cannot be saved." **(ACTS 15:1)**

Many are under the misconception that salvation by circumcision was a teaching of God in the Old Testament. Before we go on, we need to understand that Moses never gave any such instruction! Salvation has never been about any single action, including circumcision. It is first a supernatural work of the Holy Spirit that then makes its way into our acts and lifestyle. What these specific Pharisees were teaching was not something founded in Torah as instructed by Moses, but a works-based teaching that is in direct opposition to the heart of God regarding the salvation of His Bride by grace through faith in Christ.

Even before Christ, Abraham was justified (gained salvation) through faith:

What then shall we say that Abraham, our forefather according to the flesh, discovered in this matter? If, in fact, Abraham was justified by works, he had something to boast about—but not before God. What does Scripture say? "Abraham believed God, and it was credited to him as righteousness." **(ROMANS 4:1-3)**

Nothing has changed. Before Christ, we were justified by faith. After Christ, we are justified by faith. So where do our works of obedience fit in? Obedience to His instructions is not the root of our salvation, but the fruit of it. To top this off, Abraham even received this salvation before he was ever circumcised physically (Romans 4:11).

In Acts 15, the Pharisees persecute gentiles by questioning their salvation in their uncircumcision, but the apostles respond that they should not burden them with this "requirement," as it is not a true requirement of salvation. In fact, it never has been! The Word of God has stated from the beginning that circumcision of the heart should take place first, and that the circumcision of the flesh is simply an outward sign of what has already occurred inside—a fruit of our salvation.

And the Lord your God will circumcise your heart and the heart of your offspring, so that you will love the Lord your God with all your heart and with all your soul, that you may live. **(DEUTERONOMY 30:6)**

Circumcise yourselves to the Lord; remove the foreskin of your hearts. **(JEREMIAH 4:4)**

The apostles of course state that they are not saved by some certain action or event, but rather by placing their faith in Yeshua the Messiah. After the apostles declare this, however, they do list a few essentials that the pagan gentiles coming into the faith need to ensure they do:

Abstain from the things polluted by idols, and from sexual immorality, and from what has been strangled, and from blood. For from ancient generations Moses has had in every city those who proclaim him, for he is read every Sabbath in the synagogues. **(ACTS 15:19)**

All of the listed elements have been taken straight from Leviticus. From sexual immorality (Leviticus 20) to the instruction on what is proper and improper to eat (Leviticus 7 and 11). He then ends it off with a peculiar statement: he tells them about the authority of Moses' writings and that it is being read in every assembly.

So first off, he lists a few essentials for the believers to follow in the beginning of their walk with Yeshua. Then he tells them they will get the rest when they assemble in the synagogues. We need to realise that the "church" they were talking about was different from most modern churches. If you were to go to a messianic (Jesus following) fellowship in that day, you would find the writings of Moses being taught—they had no New Testament!

All scripture is given by inspiration of God, and is profitable for doctrine, for reproof, for correction, for instruction in righteousness. **(2 TIMOTHY 3:16)**

As I said before, the **only** "scripture" Timothy could be referring to was the front of your book—the Torah given by God as a love letter to His Bride. If the front of your book is profitable for doctrine and correction, why do we get angry when corrected by it, or even avoid it altogether?

From this we can deduce that legalism can originate in only two ways:

- When we twist scripture into a justified-by-works gospel, a doctrine that has never been the heart of the Father (e.g. salvation by circumcision)
- When we place man-made laws as a requirement for salvation (e.g. the laws on washing of hands)

When we place any extra, man-made law on the shoulders of men for them to do to gain salvation, we have adopted the Pharisee spirit and are burdening people with tradition.

We need to be very clear that what we are talking about in this book is not about salvation. We are talking about something deeper. We are talking about being saved by grace through faith, while running after holiness and away from lawlessness:

Therefore leaving the principles of the doctrine of Christ, let us go on unto perfection; not laying again the foundation of repentance from dead works, and of faith toward God, Of the doctrine of baptisms, and of laying on of hands, and of resurrection of the dead, and of eternal judgment.
(HEBREWS 6:1-2)

It's time to get past the basics. Many Christians are still in the mindset that salvation is the finish line, instead of realizing that salvation is just the whistle that blows at the start of the race. This is why Paul calls us to run the race so that we many finish it (1 Corinthians 9:24). Are you truly running?

And I will walk at liberty: for I seek thy precepts.
(PSALM 119:45)

THE SABBATH
The instruction that changed my life

One of the most impactful revelations revealed to me early in my walk of rediscovering the truth was the Sabbath day. This is one of the instructions given by the Father that has blessed me the most. Yet in my walk I've spoken to many who call it an abolished burden. How can there be such a disconnect?

Whenever there is confusion around anything in Scripture, we need to pause and take a deeper look in scripture with prayer. Confusion is caused by the enemy, not by God, and it is the primary indicator of the enemy's attack on something set-apart to God. This shouldn't be a surprise, for the first thing God called set-apart in Scripture was the seventh day that He rested on:

And on the seventh day God ended his work which he had made; and he rested on the seventh day from all his work which he had made. And God blessed the seventh day, and **sanctified** it: because that in it he had rested from all his work which God created and made.
(GENESIS 2:2-3, EMPHASIS ADDED)

The word sanctified ("qadash"; Strongs H6942) means to dedicate, declare holy and set-apart, appoint or purify. And as part of creating the universe, the Father set apart a very specific day and appointed it as holy. Because the Father lifts His Word above His own name and walks in obedience to it, He proves this creation by resting on it Himself. Wow! The Creator of the universe—the One who creates rest yet doesn't require rest—creates a special day and rests on it Himself. But why?

The Father has always been trying to set an example for His children. In creation, God rested on the seventh day, and when He appeared in the flesh to walk out the perfect example for us to imitate, He rested yet again.

Yes! Yeshua was in complete obedience to the Sabbath, the fourth commandment as given by Moses. For if Yeshua were not obedient, He would have been in sin and unable to die for the sins of the world as a spotless lamb. For sin is the transgression of the law (1 John 3:4).

In multiple accounts of Yeshua's ministry, He was severely persecuted for "breaking the Sabbath," according to some Pharisees. From healing on the Sabbath to picking grain on the Sabbath to working on the Sabbath, and many other accusations. It does seem that He broke the commandment, but let's take a closer look. As discussed in the previously section ("Legalism"), one form of legalism is when we attempt to work for our salvation by following the teachings and commandments of men. The Pharisees in Scripture were notoriously guilty of this. Yeshua repeatedly rebuked them for laying "heavy burdens, hard to bear, on the shoulders of others" but not even trying to lift them with their own fingers (Matthew 23:4). They taught their own man-made commandments as the commandments of God and pushed aside the commandments of God through their tradition:

Making the word of God of none effect through your tradition, which ye have delivered: and many such like things do ye. **(MARK 7:13)**

Whenever Scripture refers to the "law," it is important to understand that the law of God was not the only law in existence. The laws of the Pharisees were in some groups just as highly esteemed as the law of God. Yeshua would never speak against the loving instructions of His Father, all given to benefit and bless us. Yeshua did not come to give us a new religion, but rather to instruct us and provide us with the perfect example of how to walk it out:

Brethren, I write no new commandment unto you, but an old commandment which ye had from the beginning. The old commandment is the word which ye have heard from the beginning. **(JOHN 2:7)**

In the beginning, God created the heaven and the earth and the seventh day (the Sabbath) on which He rested. As the story goes, the enemy has been attempting since the garden to destroy that which God declared as holy and good. It is time to restore all things.

One of the ways the enemy attempts to do this is to introduce a truth, but mix it with a lie. This is what causes confusion. Certain Pharisees had some truth—they wanted to keep the Sabbath day as instructed by the Father, but they mixed it with multiple lies on how to keep it, thus adding instructions not from God's Torah:

And he entered again into the synagogue; and there was a man there which had a withered hand. And they watched him, whether he would heal him on the sabbath day; that they might accuse him. And he saith unto the man which had the withered hand, Stand forth. And he saith unto them, Is it lawful to do good on the sabbath days, or to do evil? to save life, or to kill?

But they held their peace. And when he had looked round about on them with anger, being grieved for the hardness of their hearts, he saith unto the man, Stretch forth thine hand. And he stretched it out: and his hand was restored whole as the other. And the Pharisees went forth, and straightway took counsel with the Herodians against him, how they might destroy him. **(MARK 3:1-6)**

After perceiving the hardness of their hearts, Yeshua wanted to teach them the goal of the law: holiness, love, and life. If we have not love, we can keep as many commandments as we want, but it means nothing before the Father. The Pharisees considered healing on the Sabbath as work, thereby "breaking" the commandment. They missed the point that all of God's instructions are designed to bring us life! Healing someone, even if it means ministerial work, is an action of love and life and fulfils the goal of the law. It is not possible to break any commandment of the Father if the goal of the law is achieved.

But Jesus answered them, My Father worketh hitherto, and I work. Therefore the Jews sought the more to kill him, because he not only had broken the sabbath, but said also that God was his Father, making himself equal with God. **(JOHN 5:17-18)**

The Father's work Yeshua referred to was the same ministry work Yeshua was involved in: bringing freedom to the captive, directing the lost, healing the brokenhearted and afflicted. These are not the secular works the Torah instructs us to refrain from on the Sabbath (Exodus 20:10). The Pharisees' accusation that Yeshua broke the Sabbath was merely their accusation and perception, according to their man-made laws.

The Sabbath commandment instructs us to do all our work on the six days of the week (Sunday – Friday), but rest on the seventh day (Saturday). While Constantine attempted to change the Sabbath to the first day (Sunday), as discussed earlier, God does not change. We can choose to rest any day we want, but God rests on the seventh day, and He instructs us to meet Him on that day.

MY DATE WITH JESUS

This is the most incredible part of this instruction. Yeshua has made a date with us, one day every week. He has been asking us if we will join Him in this intimacy to get to know Him better, to love Him and follow Him. We understand the importance of spending time with our spouses, to get to know them—spending long hours of the night speaking to and loving each other. Yet we believe we can be in a relationship with the Creator without setting one day a week aside for Him. He is much more vast and endless than our earthly relationships. How much time He deserves considering what He has given us!

The Sabbath is my 24-hour date with Yeshua. It's the day I tell the world to get behind me, because it's time for my King! He gets top priority. And I'm not the only one who shows up for that "date"—He shows up too, for He is still resting on the seventh day.

The Sabbath is a day to spend time with the Father and fellowship with our brothers and sisters in scripture, prayer, worship, etc. It's the day that fathers give time to their family—everyone (especially wives) can have a rest, and children are prayed for and blessed. We prepare for the day in advance by making sure we won't need to buy groceries, work hard at making food, etc. We prepare to enter His rest! When Sunday comes, I hope for Saturday (Sabbath), and when Sabbath comes, the highlight of my week has arrived, because it's time for Yeshua to invade my home with peace.

The Sabbath has been one of the number one instructions that has not only accelerated and drawn me much closer to the Father in intimacy, but has also grown my faith. While keeping the Sabbath has now become second-nature and part of my lifestyle, it wasn't always this way. The first month of changing my life to start keeping the instruction— changing work schedules or saying no to certain events held on Saturdays—was not easy.

When Israel started observing the Sabbath in the Exodus, God asked them to gather their manna on the first six days of the week, and said that He would provide enough manna on day six to sustain them during day seven (Exodus 16:22). When they disobeyed, the manna they worked to gather on the seventh day was rotten. Keeping the Sabbath is a great test of faith that all who are not keeping the instruction will never learn. The reality is many do not keep this instruction, despite the excuses, due to their own unbelief. We do not believe that God will provide enough manna on the six days to sustain us for the seventh.

Bob, a restaurant owner, just discovered the Sabbath day. Saturdays are his prime time of business, but Bob believed the Scriptures and nervously decided to shut down his business on the busiest day of the week to be obedient. The numbers said his business would fail if he did so, but he believes God. In this true story, Bob's business made more money in the first month of following the Sabbath than ever before!

Similarly, when I started observing the commandment during my university career, it was a great test of faith. On one occasion in my first year of studies, a Monday morning exam was approaching. As I started preparing for the examination, I realised I started preparing too late. As the weekend approached, I honoured the Sabbath day and rejoiced in it with the Father, forgetting about my work and focussing on Him. By the end of Sunday's preparation for the exam, I realised I would be able to get to only around half of the work required to prepare well. I came to realise that the only hope I had to pass was in the promise of God that He will provide enough manna on the six days to sustain unto the seventh, despite my lack of preparation.

In the exam, I received the highest score of my year: 79 percent. From there, in the unwavering faith it created within me, I went on to excel in all the work I committed my hands to throughout university and into the workplace, against all odds of my under-qualification or lacking human skills. Seeing God come through miraculously and gloriously over and over again was one of the main builders of faith to make me who I am in Yeshua today. This led up to the great event that God worked in my life to be told in chapter two of this book.

WRITTEN ON THE HEART

Because the Torah is written on our hearts (Jeremiah 31:31), it often cries out and convicts our new creation to keep it in obedience. It manifests in us by creating a longing to keep it, but because we have a lack of knowledge, we don't always know how. Many believers with a close relationship with the Father will say that they want to "spend more time with God," as their spirit eagerly yearns for it. When they discover the seventh day God has set apart for this desire to be accommodated, they are often told by their spiritual leadership that it is "abolished" or "not for today." The internal confusion caused by this mixing of the truth on their heart with the lies of men sometimes causes the individual to blindly trust their pastors and forsake the fourth commandment.

But you know something isn't right. Something is missing—you know there needs to be something more. The Sabbath is only the beginning of rediscovering the Torah written on our hearts, crying out to our inner being to become obedient and walk after the perfect example of Yeshua.

If thou turn away thy foot from the sabbath, from doing thy pleasure on my holy day; and call the sabbath a delight, the holy of the LORD, honourable; and shalt honour him, not doing thine own ways, nor finding thine own pleasure, nor speaking thine own words: Then shalt thou delight thyself in the LORD; and I will cause thee to ride upon the high places of the earth, and feed thee with the heritage of Jacob thy father: for the mouth of the LORD hath spoken it. **(ISAIAH 58:13-14)**

After we take a small step of obedience towards this, God will open the gates of revelation to water our souls unto the fullness of Yeshua. We will no longer feed on mere milk, but now solid food (1 Corinthians 3:2).

REASONS FOR OBEDIENCE

In my race, many on the sidelines have come up to me and said, "Why are you running by these rules? Don't you know it brings death?"

I started realizing the idea that following God's Torah brings death is a common one among many groups. I don't follow His law because I feel damned if I don't; I don't follow His law because I want to make myself holy; and I don't follow His law because people are looking.

I follow His law because it's who I am. I follow His law because He has set me apart as holy, and so I will continue in it. I follow His law because He is watching. Above all, I follow His law because I LOVE HIM. Because I love Him, I love His Word, I love His walk, I love His Ways, and I can't get enough of Him. I will walk as He walked; I will run the race. God said, "If you love me, keep my commandments" (John 14:15). He continues to say that the one who says "I know Him" but does not keep His commandments is a liar and the truth is not in Him (1 John 2:4).

So God explains that the way you follow the most important commandment of them all (loving God) is by doing what He said. You cannot keep the first commandment without the rest of the Torah.

Apart from my motivation, the Father lays out many more reasons to follow Him. He promises blessing instead of curses, life instead of death (Deuteronomy 30:19), health instead of sickness (Deuteronomy 7:15); He promises that we will ride on heights of the nations (Isaiah 58:14); that our children will never forsake the Lord (Proverbs 22:16); that it will teach us how to love others (Leviticus 19:18); and many more reasons. These are only a few explained in detail throughout His Torah and Prophets, and all of them have been true for my life. I have never been more free from all forms of sin and bondage. I have received a blessing of boldness in Him that few ever encounter. I have seen the blind see, the lame walk, and the demon leave.

Am I saying that if everyone just studies the Torah that they will see these things? Not necessarily. Many study the Torah, inherit some of the blessings God promises through it, yet never see the fruit and power of the Spirit working in their life. Without the Spirit, the Word becomes impossible to correctly keep and apply to your life. But if you have the Spirit—and now bring the Truth to it—the miracles, power, signs, wonders, fruits of the Spirit, discernment, and other gifts are brought to its fullness. For the Spirit follows the Truth, and the Truth is empowered by the Spirit. (Note: In the next chapter of this book, I will be discussing the Spirit of God.)

According to statistics, if you are the average Christian, you have never read and studied through the entire front of your book. I would like to ask you with a burning heart to get in there. No matter how long you've been a believer, start in the beginning (Genesis), and deeply study the very Word that became flesh and came to die for our sins. After a year of doing so, you will never be the same. You will reignite the truth that God has long ago written on your heart.

LOVING THE LAW

We all know David as the man "after God's own heart" (Acts 13:22). When I heard of this incredible statement of God, I was starstruck. I want to be that, I thought, and who wouldn't want to be? The reality is, most of us want things, but not many of us are willing to illustrate that desire through action (shema). There is a very simple and clear reason that God declared such a blessed statement over David. It wasn't because of David's faith alone, or that David was a "good person" alone, but because his heart was to guard and keep the truth no matter what.

Psalm 119 (by David) is the longest chapter in your Bible. It is one of the most hated chapters in your Bible by the kingdom of darkness as well. This chapter illustrates the inner thoughts and David's love for God. First I thought, How could God love a man this much? Then, when I read what David wrote, I thought, How could David have such a love for God? You start witnessing an incredible relationship between Father Yahweh and son:

With my whole heart have I sought thee: O let me not wander from thy **commandments**. Thy word have I hid in mine heart, that I might not sin against thee.
(PSALM 119:10-11, EMPHASIS ADDED)

Open thou mine eyes, that I may behold wondrous things out of thy **law** [Torah]. I am a stranger in the earth: hide not thy **commandments** from me.
(PSALM 119:18-19, EMPHASIS ADDED)

Thou hast rebuked the proud that are cursed, which do err from thy **commandments**.
(PSALM 119:21, EMPHASIS ADDED)

Remove from me the way of lying: and grant me thy **law** graciously. I have chosen the way of **truth**: thy **judgments** have I laid before me. **(PSALM 119:29-30, EMPHASIS ADDED)**

Give me understanding, and I shall keep thy **law**; yea, I shall observe it with my whole heart. Make me to go in the path of thy **commandments**; for therein do I **delight**.
(PSALM 119:34-35, EMPHASIS ADDED)

And take not the word of **truth** utterly out of my mouth; for I have hoped in thy **judgments**. So shall I keep thy **law** continually for ever and ever. And I will walk at **liberty**: for I seek thy **precepts. (PSALM 119:43-45, EMPHASIS ADDED)**

We only picked a few of the 176 verses that I encourage you to read. You won't hear Psalm 119 read in over half of modern churches, because it opposes all "hyper-grace" doctrine that teaches against God's law. For the enemy to succeed, he realises that he needs to change definitions of what truth is. We have continually read that the Torah of God is truth:

Thy righteousness is an everlasting righteousness, and thy Torah is the truth. **(PSALM 119:142)**

In the garden, the enemy questioned, "Did God really mean that?" And today the enemy is still questioning: "Did God really mean you need to keep all His instructions? Isn't it a burden?" Recognize that voice? It's time to expose the darkness with the light. Psalm 119 forms a powerful part of that light. I realised after reading this psalm that there is honestly **no more excuse**. We can choose ignorance of the truth—stay comfortable in our current belief—or we can humble ourselves, pray, and repent before the Father.

For many of us, this is a difficult realisation to come to terms with, and convincing ourselves otherwise by picking and choosing the scriptures we would like to read and believe will not make it right. God is finishing up; this age of lawlessness will soon pass away and all will appear before His throne. The books are opened and our works are assessed. Assessed against what? The Torah. The Torah written on your heart will testify of your works—not only in obedience, but in intentions of obedience. The pastor will not be there to save you from God's wrath. He might in fact be forced to testify against your lukewarmness in reading the Word for yourself. If you have trampled underfoot the son of God by denying the instructions the Son has come to fill up, you will have no inheritance.

The trumpet will blow any day now. And when you hear it, time will be up. There will be no second chance to check yourself and repent. There will be no one between you and the wrath of God. "Oh what a fearful thing it is to fall into the hands of the living God!" (Hebrews 10:31). But for those who have the right garment on—a spotless garment cleansed by the blood of Yeshua that sealed the Torah written on their heart—it will be a glorious day.

God is looking for men and women "after His own heart." We know what satisfies our Father's heart. It is time. It is time to step into the fullness of Yeshua's walk without excuse. No more denominations, no more changing of definitions or picking and choosing, but pure imitation of our Messiah.

After all, if we love Him, we will keep His commandments (John 14:15)

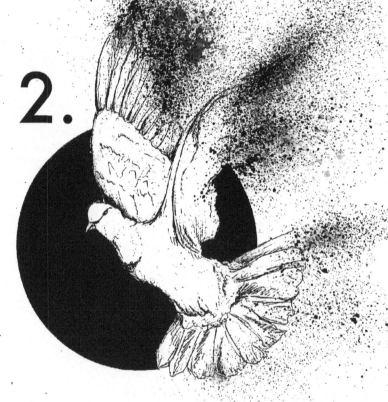

REIGNITING
SPIRIT

2.

Reigniting Spirit

For truly, I say to you, many prophets and righteous people longed to see what you see, and did not see it, and to hear what you hear, and did not hear it. **(MATTHEW 13:17)**

We are entering the most important season the world has long awaited. The Scriptures say that lawlessness will increase as we near the end of the age, and as we approach the end of this age. It calls for the people of God to enter a place of faith and obedience that surpasses all generations before it—even the first disciples.

The point of this book is not to explore different directions of how the end times may play out. But I believe we can all agree that there will come a great time of trouble for those who call themselves a "follower of Jesus/Yeshua." The world already hates (and will increase its hate towards) the remnant. Most don't know this, but according to the *Center for Studies on New Religions*, one believer is killed every six minutes due to proclaiming his or her faith. While already being the most persecuted group in the world, there will come a time when this number will go up, and God's people will have a greater type of Exodus journey through perilous times. This wilderness experience will be worse than the first Exodus; and will prove our faith and foundations to breaking point.

Dear brother or sister, you need to understand that a storm is coming—a mighty display of God's power that the world has not seen since the time of the great flood. There will be blood and fire and columns of smoke; the creation will submit to only the Father, and those who run will have no place to hide. However, even though times will be dire, the true Bride of Christ will be under His wing. But this remnant will not be your average lukewarm Christian. There will be an incredible work of

Spirit and Truth preparation that God has worked in them long before the storm hits. If you knew a mighty storm was coming, would you not prepare? Would you not do what is necessary to survive it? Yet the people of God have been lukewarm and passive over the prophesied storm of Revelation.

You will be either an observer or partaker of this storm. An observer will be swept away by it; a partaker will battle by the side of Yeshua in this end-time battle for the last souls.

You cannot partake in this battle against the darkness if you have no weapons. Today, most of those God has chosen to endure until the end have been stripped of their weapons by the enemy. He has succeeded in making us believe that these weapons are not for today or the future, but that the time to use them is long over; that they are completely irrelevant to the Kingdom or call of God; that they are not for us, or that we are not worthy to use them. The enemy knows that he stands no chance against God's army, but he knows he can buy time by disarming the people of God by his lies.

In the following section, I pray that the Father will restore your Sword of the Spirit and other weapons necessary for warfare to you, to make you fit and able for battle. Many think this storm has yet to hit, or that this battle has yet to begin, but I submit to you today that we are already witnessing the beginning of the great last move of God.

MARKS OF SHAVUOT
Mount Sinai & Mount Zion

God's Festival of Weeks (also known as Pentecost—Shavuot in He-brew) "marks" two of the most important events in history. It is at this festival that God chose to equip His Bride with the two elements she needs to walk in the fullness of Him. I call these two events the "marks of Shavuot."

A dark cloud—thick darkness covered the mountain. The sound of trumpets pierced the air. A ferocious fire consumed the mountain Moses stood on, and the rocks vibrated. The children of Israel beheld the glory of God, **stood far off**, and were very afraid (Exodus 20:18).

With every Word spoken, a mighty rushing wind threw itself across the crowds. The trees bowed with every blow, and the fire grew with every Word. "Moses, you speak to God, lest we die!" the people shouted **(EXODUS 20:19).**

At the time of Shavuot, God appeared and gave the Bride His perfect instructions (Exodus 24:13, Psalm 19:7) on Mount Sinai. In their fear of the pure presence, glory, and work of God on the mountain, they asked Moses to talk to God for their sake. Fear was what kept them from be-holding the Father's work face-to-face. They rejected the outpouring of God's Spirit and were given a human mediator. Because of this, they were not able to enter the same intimacy and walk of power possible today. The instructions were written on stone for them, instructions that opposed their being and sinful nature. Following the event, they attempted to worship God in their own carnal ways and built a golden calf. Three thousand of them died that day as a result (Exodus 32:28).

1200 years later on Mount Zion, the second historical "mark" occurs at the festival of Shavuot. The apostles assembled in one accord in the Temple, as per the Father's instructions (Deuteronomy 16:16), and also per Yeshua's instructions to not leave Jerusalem (Acts 1:4). As they start-ed praying, a slight breeze entered the Temple gate. They could hear the soothing sound of the dancing trees. But suddenly, a mighty rushing wind entered. They experienced a fire running right through them, causing them to give utterance to unknown tongues. Many came from far-away places to assemble for Shavuot in that day (Acts 2:1, Deuteronomy 16:16). And when they saw this, they **drew near** to them, and were astounded that they could each hear in their own language. Three thousand were baptized in the pools and added to the Kingdom on that day (Acts 2:41).

At this event, Shavuot makes another mark in history, 1200 years removed from the giving of the instructions on Mount Sinai—a hundred years for each of the 12 tribes. The Father poured out His Spirit on all flesh at Mount Zion, and three thousand people received the Spirit. Both of these events occurred on mountains (Mount Sinai and Mount Zion) during Shavuot. The three thousand who fell at Mount Sinai because of the golden calf are paralleled by the three thousand saved on Mount Zion.

As the first gift, the Father gave His perfect Torah (truth); as the second, He gave His Spirit. In the giving of His truth, the people beheld His glory—fire, wind, and thick darkness—and drew away **in fear**. But at Mount Zion, the people were **not afraid** but drawn to it.

Many today in the Truth Group who graciously follow His instructions have become afraid of the workings of the Holy Spirit. Instead of facing God face-to-face, we have opted to view Him only through the Scriptures. While viewing God through the Scriptures is a wonderful and necessary element in our journey of knowing Him, it is only a part of the process. Without coming to the Father face-to-face, His glow does not emanate from our faces. The Spirit of God enables the fruits, power, and love Yeshua walked in. Without the fullness of the Spirit, we may have good theology, but only a half-baked walk.

How amazing that God orchestrated both of these events to take place on mountains. There is good reason for this. I've told you how I fell to my knees and begged God for **truth**—a secret-place moment that changed my life and walk forever. It was my Mount Sinai experience of receiving His Torah.

After receiving His Torah, I started applying it to my life. I thought I was pretty good at applying His commandments to my walk and being obedient. But if I'm honest with myself, I struggled. I struggled loving the way Yeshua loved. I didn't care for the poor, the widow, or the orphan; I didn't cast out demons; I didn't see the sick get healed. In fact, I don't think there was anything "supernatural" about my life at all. I remember asking a messianic (Yeshua believing) Jewish friend, "Why don't we see these things?" He was honest and simply said he didn't know. Many others told me that they "ceased" or that they are still "working towards it." They believed that, one day, they will be holy enough to see God work something similar in them. I was left frustrated, because there was this part of my Messiah's walk that was instructed yet seemed unattainable.

The 1200 year gap between the giving of Truth (Mount Sinai) and the giving of His Spirit (Mount Zion) tells an important story. Each of us begins with a greater measure of one or the other, and maturing each one is an important process. Most people mature either Spirit or Truth, but rarely both. We were all created with a tendency. Some people are very much driven by logic and reason, while others are driven more by emotion, feeling, or "spirituality." Neither of these tendencies is wrong— they both are designed to give glory to God. But either one can be dangerous when used by the enemy.

You will see people tending to logic and reason often turning into atheists, and you will see many people tending to emotion or spirituality turning to the new age movement or occultism. Furthermore, you will see many religious men who study the Truth without the Spirit deny the Messiah, because knowledge without fruit congests within and puffs up. A puffed-up man doesn't seem to need a saviour. This is the "leaven of the Pharisees" (Matthew 16:6). On the other hand, many religious men with the Spirit but without the Truth may do a miracle, but they are destroyed for their lack of knowledge of the Truth, which leads to the error of the lawless. These are some of the ultimate consequences of tipping the pendulum too far.

After five years of maturing in the Truth I received, I fell on my knees again. This time, the Father would do something even bigger than the first time, to bring about my Mount Zion (Spirit) experience.

He would do something in my life that would change me, challenge others, and bring a great restoration of Spirit in my life. (At least I didn't need to wait 1200 years.)

Before I tell you what happened, I would like to express the significance of falling on your knees. Mountains played an important role in the Bible. We have established that Spirit and Truth were given on mountains by God, but we also read how Yeshua often departed from His disciples to pray on mountains, and even met with Moses and Elijah on the mountain.

MOUNT OF TRANSFIGURATION & YESHUA'S BAPTISM

The mount of transfiguration and Yeshua's baptism are two more events that mark the fulfillment of the two outpourings of Spirit & Truth.

And it came to pass about an eight days after these sayings, he took Peter and John and James, and went up into a mountain to pray. **(LUKE 9:28)**

Moses and Elijah appeared to Yeshua and His disciples. Moses represents the Torah, as the Torah was given through Moses; and Elijah represents the Prophets.

Similar to Mount Sinai, a cloud covered the mountain and Yeshua's face shone like the face of Moses. The disciples fell to their faces (as the Israelites on Mount Sinai) and the Father spoke, "This is My Son, the Beloved. Hear Him!" (Luke 9:35). The Father confirms the fullness, glory, and unity of Yeshua with Truth (Torah & Prophets) and says that we need to hear and follow His example. This is why Yeshua is greater than Moses, and greater than Elijah: He is the fulfillment and goal of both the Torah and the Prophets, as He is the One they both point towards.

Yeshua was not greater than Moses because Moses was wrong, nor greater than Elijah because Elijah was wrong. He was greater because both are right and they were both right within Him. The mount of transfiguration was a type of "ordination ceremony." Moses and Elijah were the two witnesses of Truth required to confirm Yeshua as high priest in the order of Melchizedek. Therefore, the Father says: "Hear Him!" confirming that what Yeshua speaks, is truth.

There is an important connection between the mount of transfiguration and the event on Mount Sinai. On Mount Sinai, we witnessed the cloud with thick darkness, followed by the voice of God and the giving of the commandments to Moses. This event was very similar to the transfiguration and was perfectly orchestrated to point to it—it has always been about Yeshua and the fulfillment of the Torah and Prophets within Him, and it all happened with the witness of Moses and Elijah. The transfiguration is Yeshua's "Mount Sinai experience."

While the transfiguration is connected to Truth, Yeshua's baptism is connected to Spirit. At Yeshua's baptism, John is hindered and feels unworthy to baptize Yeshua (Matthew 3:14), but Yeshua says:

And Jesus answering said unto him, Suffer it to be so now: for thus it becometh us to **fulfil all righteousness**. Then he suffered him. **(MATTHEW 3:15, EMPHASIS ADDED)**

As Yeshua came up from the water, the heavens opened, and the Spirit of God descended upon Him as a dove. From the heavens, God spoke and declared: "This is my beloved Son, in whom I am well pleased" **(MATTHEW 3:17)**

This was Yeshua's "Mount Zion experience", or rather what Mount Zion experienced with the outpouring of the Spirit. When the Spirit descended upon the disciples during the festival of Shavuot (Pentecost) on Mount Zion, 3000 came to faith in Yeshua as their Messiah and were then baptized.

While Moses and Elijah were the witnesses of the Torah and Prophets at the mount of transfiguration, John was the witness of the Spirit. As John was hesitant, Yeshua told him this must happen for Him to "fulfil all righteousness." To understand what He meant, we need to understand that John is of the bloodline of the Levitical priesthood, as both parents of John the Baptist were descendants of Aaron (from the tribe of Levi). The role of the Levitical priests was to facilitate man's appearance before God, by coming before the Spirit of God in the temple once a year at the Day of Atonement. The Levitical priests were witnesses of the Spirit.

Before the ordination of new Levitical priests, a mikvah (type of baptism) was done as part of the ordination ceremony. John, a true Levitical priest (a witness of Spirit), is called to baptize Yeshua because this is another ordination ceremony of Yeshua as a priest of Melchizedek. The first ordination was with the witness of John (Spirit), the second was with the witness of Moses and Elijah (Torah and Prophets/Truth).

Therefore, we see the mount of transfiguration is the fulfillment of the giving of the commandments at Mount Sinai, and Yeshua's baptism is the fulfillment of the giving of the Spirit in the Levitical temples; and the Spirit indwells Yeshua's temple as Holy Spirit descends upon Him like a dove.

At the mount of transfiguration, God speaks: "This is My Son, the Beloved. Hear Him!" as a witness of Truth; while at Yeshua's baptism, God speaks: "This is my beloved Son, in whom I am well pleased." as a witness of Spirit. The truth within us causes what we say to be heard by those who believe and know the truth, while the Spirit within us is what allows us to have faith and walk out that truth in a manner God is pleased in.

By these events, we clearly see the golden thread of Spirit & Truth that travel the pages of our Bibles. God has designed the Truth to direct the Spirit from the beginning, and the Spirit to empower the Truth. Yeshua was the first example ever given that provides us with the fullness of God's plan of Spirit & Truth for our life and walk.

MY MOUNT ZION EXPERIENCE

The only way for you to also receive the fullness of Spirit and Truth is to absolutely die to yourself—your ways, your previous beliefs, your assumptions, your fears, your insecurities—and give control to Him. False doctrine, pride, and fear are the biggest reasons people never walk in the fullness of Christ. You need to fall on your face, like I did. You need to say, "No matter what the price of Spirit and Truth is, I want all of it." You need to be willing to lose everything for His sake.

This is exactly what I did next. I begged God for His Spirit, and shortly thereafter I received a dream. I had never received a dream from God before. I had no framework, but this is what I saw.

I was standing in a marketplace within the streets of Jerusalem. Many people were moving between the stalls of food. There was a small boy in front of me, and in front of him was a small girl. I told the boy to lay his hand on her shoulder and command the pain to leave her. Afterwards, she raised her arm and got completely healed! She turned around and ran away, only to come back with her Jewish mother. I told her, "This was all Yeshua!" Next, transported to another place in the dream, I'm running from heavy persecution through the streets and rooftops of Jerusalem amongst a few other believing brothers and sisters.

Then I woke up. I had never really prayed for anyone, never had a dream of God, and didn't even know if this was from Him. But the dream stirred something inside me, and the next week I fasted and prayed for revelation if this was from Him.

A week later, I'm sitting in my apartment one night and feel a voice tell me, "Go to Hatfield Square. There's someone you need to meet." It wasn't audible, but more of a mix between a thought, a feeling, and "knowing." At the moment I had no idea what was going on, and this voice didn't leave me. I felt that I must be going crazy, but I got in my car and drove to Hatfield Square, an area not far off. As soon as I parked and got out of my car, a man walked up to me and started talking to me about his life. It was a seemingly random encounter. A power and boldness suddenly came over me and I blurted out, "Hey, random question—do you have pain your shoulder?"

The man looked bewildered and nodded his head. "Yes, why?" I said, "Jesus is going to take all that pain right now!" As soon as I said it, I couldn't believe what I was doing. I was so afraid, and although the things I said and did were within my control, I knew this wasn't me. I laid my hands on his shoulder, and I commanded all the pain to leave.

"Lift up your arm, test it out," I told him. I didn't want to leave not knowing what had happened. I was pretty new at this, uncertain and somewhat skeptic. He lifted his arm slowly, and immediately dropped it again. "The pain is gone!" He lifted it over and over and was deeply searching for the pain he just felt moments before. He looked at me and said seriously, "Wait here, I'm bringing someone to you." Moments later, he brings his friend who is struggling to walk and asks me to pray for his foot. *Let's just try this again,* I thought, laying my hand on his foot. "I command this foot to be restored completely. All pain get out now!" He applied pressure to his foot, and all pain left again—completely.

They started directing me to their friends who had issues, and people were being directed to me. I started praying for legs, back issues, teeth, and just about everything you could think of. When I finished one person, I turned around and there was another. By the end of the night, I had prayed for around 25 people, all of them being healed physically. I even had a demon-possessed man come and pull me off someone I was praying for. I looked at him and said, "Go, in the name of Jesus," and he ran away immediately.

Now I'd like to stress something. This wasn't me. Before this, I had never seen a physical miracle, and I had barely prayed for a stranger before. The best way I can describe that night's experience is that I was on "autopilot." I was fully in control and fully conscious, but also so filled and led by the Spirit that He worked through me in a supernatural way. I believe Yeshua experienced this same nature in His walk. This is a large part of being "led by the Spirit." It starts with submission to the Truth and submission to the Spirit—dying to yourself—trading what seems right to a man for what is right to God, and your nature for His nature.

This only would I learn of you, Received ye the Spirit by the works of the law, or by the hearing of faith? **(GALATIANS 3:2)**

It is not something I attained by working for it or by being holy enough. God isn't up there waiting for us to meet some criteria of holiness and perfection before He gives us His Spirit. He gives it despite our imperfection. If He required perfection before using us, He would never be able to work through any of us, nor fill any of us with His Set-Apart Spirit. For we all have fallen short of the glory of God (Romans 3:23)—just in different areas. Thinking that our issues are less serious to God than the imperfection of others is self-righteousness rooted in pride. Self-righteousness, pride, and the belief that they need to "work" for the Spirit are the three main reasons we find true believers who have a form of knowledge, know the Truth of the Word, but remain powerless against the forces of darkness. Therefore we see people following His instructions, but not walking in the power that Yeshua walked and commanded us to walk in.

I drove home crying that night. I was wrecked. I knew that my life was changed forever. The next day I went to the university in awe. I told everyone I could find. I walked up to crippled people and, by the power and grace of Yeshua, I left them walking. I say this not to boast, but to boast in Him—to demonstrate the immediate change the power of the Holy Spirit can work in one's life. You don't need to wait 30 years to accomplish this; you just need one night and the belief of a child.

Most people I told were excited for me, but I wasn't satisfied by this. I didn't want them excited for me—I wanted them excited for the Kingdom. In the car while driving home that night, the Father whispered, "Now go, I want all My people to walk in this." The people I told were mostly not interested in applying this to their life or walking in this. I don't think they did not desire it, but that they feared it. Fear of what others think, fear of failure, and the inability to humble yourself are all crafted tactics of the enemy to create a passivity of the works of the Spirit in your life.

Right before Yeshua's ascension, He starts off by reproaching the disciples for their unbelief in His resurrection. It is interesting that the Messiah used this as the introduction to the Great Commission:

Later He appeared to the eleven as they sat at the table. And He reproached their unbelief and hardness of heart, because they did not believe those who had seen Him after He was raised. And He said to them, "Go into all the world and proclaim the Good News to every creature."
(MARK 16:14-15 ISR)

It is important to note that these are some of the last, most important instructions given by our Saviour before ascending. He could have told them many things, but He opted to remind them of this will of the Father. He then continues to state that there are going to be a few signs that will mark those who **believe**:

And these signs shall follow them that believe; In my name shall they cast out devils; they shall speak with new tongues; They shall take up serpents; and if they drink any deadly thing, it shall not hurt them; they shall lay hands on the sick, and they shall recover. So then after the Lord had spoken unto them, he was received up into heaven, and sat on the right hand of God. **(MARK 16:17-19)**

First, our messiah outlined the unbelief of the disciples. Then He tells them that signs will accompany those who believe. But why does He do this? It's simple. He is demonstrating that they need to simply believe. Why, oh crooked generation, do you doubt? We can have all the knowledge of His Word, spend countless hours on mission fields, disciple tens and preach to thousands, and we will have good fruit—but if we don't believe that what He said in Mark 16, we will never see these signs accompany us. And because of this, we will never be able to walk in the fullness of our callings.

Belief is not a feeling, its is an action. Often, we are led by our feelings and come to believe our feelings of doubt and allow them to discourage us. However, Yeshua told them to do these things despite their unbelief because He knew that if only they go out into the world and **do**, then all the necessary belief is demonstrated and existent for the Spirit to move and signs to follow.

I have frequently had feelings of doubt in the midst of the greatest miracles, but I understand its not about what I feel, it's about what I do.

It's Judgement Day, and it's your turn. As you walk up to the front of the court, your heart is pounding at His majesty, and fear of the unknown—what will be written in the books? You appear before the Father, and the Book of Works (Revelation 20:12) is opened. He begins by praising your good works: you taught many the truth of His word. On the mission field, He shows a list of the names of people saved through your life's example. He also notes your name is in the Book of Life. It's like a heavy weight just lifted off your shoulders. But before it's over, the Father starts talking about the person you could have been.

"Do you remember the blind man you sat next to on the bus?" You immediately recall this blind man. While sitting next to him one day, you spoke to him about God. You grieved for his loss of sight. In your heart you knew the Father was telling you to pray for him. But you never did, because you felt like you had no belief. *I don't have the gift*, you thought. In the courtroom, the Father shows a different reality, where you got up and prayed for the blind man while the entire bus was looking. God opens his eyes and, before the bus reaches its destination, people are crying in repentance. Amongst one of the people was an atheist who would fulfil his calling to become a great missionary that would lead millions to Christ in Africa. But this never happened, because you were afraid of what others might think.

Jesus answered, "It was not that this [blind] man sinned, or his parents, but that the works of God might be displayed in him." **(JOHN 9:3)**

"That man was blind for My glory to manifest. Because you did not welcome My Spirit, but despised My supernatural works, I was never able to work in the fullness of your life's calling. You were effective, but also misunderstood **who you were**. And because you misunderstood who you were, you took away from My glory, for you are made in my image."

Most true believers do not walk in the fullness of Spirit for the same reason they might not walk in the fullness of Truth: a lack of knowledge, either of Scripture itself or who they are in light of Scripture.

And I will give you shepherds according to mine heart, which shall feed you with knowledge and understanding.
(JEREMIAH 3:15)

God is bringing forth a mighty restoration of Spirit and Truth to His bride to walk in the fullness of Yeshua's walk. In the previous chapter, we talked about the return to obedience, holiness, and His instructions. This is a restoration of knowledge, but it is not the end of the story or the full picture, only half of it. After the giving of truth at Shavuot on Mount Sinai, a restoration of that truth has started in these last days. Similarly, now 2000 years after the giving of the Spirit at Shavuot (Pentecost) on Mount Zion, a restoration of knowledge is required in terms of His Spirit too.

THE HOLY SPIRIT
Your Identity in Spirit

Holy Spirit is called *Ruach HaKodesh* in Hebrew. Ruach means "breath" or "wind" (Strongs 7307), while kodesh means "holy" or "set apart" (Strongs 6944).

If God has filled you with His Spirit, you need to understand what that means. He breathed (ruach) His Set-Apart Spirit into you. He did not give us a little bit of the Holy Spirit, or a different version than that of old. The same Spirit of God that dwelled in and led the Messiah and the disciples was sent by Him to now dwell in us. The Holy Spirit did not change the way He does things, for He changes not (Malachi 3:6).

This is critical to believe and understand, for if you believe that Yeshua did not give you what He promised—a promise that will enable you to proclaim the gospel to all creation—then you will never accomplish it.

But if the Spirit of him that raised up Jesus from the dead dwell in you, he that raised up Christ from the dead shall also quicken your mortal bodies by his Spirit that dwelleth in you.
(ROMANS 8:11)

This all means that the fullness of God is now able to live and work in and through us. This is major. It means that when you walk into that grocery store with the hurting cashier, it's no longer you that needs to save her. In fact, you are so small in relation to the Holy Spirit of God that "you" shouldn't even be in this picture. Your flesh is only as significant in the realm of evangelism as you want it to be—and preferably, we want none of our flesh involved.

CARNAL MIND VS. SPIRIT

Our flesh is the biggest tool in the enemy's hand against us.

The Scriptures state that the carnal mind (flesh) is at enmity with God and not subject to the law of God, nor can it be (Romans 8:7). Our carnal mind forms a big part of our fallen nature. It rebels against all His ways, callings, and desires for our lives and favours the ways of the world instead—evil pleasures, selfishness, anger, hatred, etc. The flesh desires only to satisfy itself, and is ruled by what feels right to a man (Proverbs 14:12).

The biggest battle remains to be against dark principalities and forces of darkness in high places (Ephesians 6:12). But instead of facing us head on, they wage war against us through this "old man"—our old nature. When Yeshua calls us to die to ourselves, he calls us to die to this old nature in favour of the new. Baptism is the tool God has gifted us with to provide a means of renewal. This means that you are not your flesh, nor are you supposed to be led by it!

Think of an elephant. Now, stop thinking of the elephant. And now, forget the elephant! You cannot change your carnal mind. Our minds were designed to keep information and learn; we cannot "erase" a memory like hitting delete on a computer. To solve this, we are buried in baptism (Romans 6:4), raised with Yeshua to become a brand new creation with a new nature. The old man dies and is buried, and you become reborn with the brand new mind, like a baby:

Nicodemus said to him, "How can a man be born when he is old? Can he enter a second time into his mother's womb and be born?" **(JOHN 3:4)**

This is why Yeshua calls us to believe "like a child." There are many "grown-ups" who try to walk in the fullness of Christ. The works of the Spirit are not against logic and reason, or truth from God, but they are against the carnal mind and that which seems right to a man. Everything the Spirit attempts will conflict with those who have not received a new mind.

When Yeshua walked on water, the disciples were terrified, and probably very weirded out. In fact, they initially thought Yeshua was a ghost (Matthew 14:26). When Yeshua casted out demons, the Pharisees said

He was doing so by the prince of demons (Matthew 9:34).
When Yeshua healed many, He was labelled a false worker of miracles.
When the Holy Spirit was poured out at Shavuot, many came to accuse those speaking in tongues as being "drunk with wine" (Acts 2:13). Have you ever felt like you just don't want to pray or do spiritual things?

In all these instances, and many more, we clearly see unrenewed, carnal minds at battle with the workings of the Spirit. We need to understand that these aren't necessarily the minds of unbelievers, but even those who have a good concept of truth (e.g. the disciples).

YOUR IDENTITY IN SPIRIT

In the Garden of Eden, Satan sold Adam and Eve a counterfeit identity, something different from what God proclaimed over them initially. Satan told them that he would make them "like God" (Genesis 3:5). Ironically, they were already made in His image (Genesis 1:27). This counterfeit identity or "seed" still has a grip on us; the world calls it human nature, but God calls the fruit of this seed an abomination.

To overcome this, we first need to understand and believe who we are. First, after baptism, the old man's nature sold to us by Satan is buried. You take upon a new identity given to you through your inheritance by faith in Yeshua (2 Corinthians 5:17).

This identity is not like the one you had before—you are now a child of the living God. You are chosen and part of a royal priesthood of a Divine Kingdom not of this world (1 Peter 2:9). This means that what people say of me no longer defines who I am, but only what He says or thinks matters. You are called to be His hands and feet, and because the Kingdom is within you, it should not be unusual for the Kingdom to manifest when you pray, speak, or walk. Instead, it should be unusual if it doesn't happen. For a bad tree cannot bear good fruit, and a good tree cannot bear bad fruit. The seed within you will determine the fruit you grow, and that seed is accessed by faith in Yeshua that brings forth a new creation with changed works:

And when he was demanded of the Pharisees, when the kingdom of God should come, he [Yeshua] answered them and said, the kingdom of God cometh not with observation: Neither shall they say, Lo here! or, lo there! for, **behold, the kingdom of God is within you.**
(LUKE 17:20-21, EMPHASIS ADDED)

Second, we need to be mindful of the carnal mind and old man. Becoming more self-aware about this will help us battle it. You cannot battle an enemy you don't even know about. When we talk about being "mindful" of the old man, we are not talking about giving him attention or authority, looking to him or living in his nature. After baptism, the enemy attempts to remind believers of who they once were; he wants us to look back and give attention to our fallen identity of the past. Therefore the first thing the enemy attempted after Yeshua was baptized, was to visit Him in the wilderness to offer Him the delicacies of the world. Yeshua calls us to walk in the new creation that is fearless, bold, follows the law written on our hearts, and inherits a clear conscience before the Father through the blood shed for our sins.

This means that, within my state of continuous repentance before the Father, nothing I do will separate me from the love of God (Romans 8:35), unless I separate myself. It means that the miracle is not dependent on my works, but His works operating through my faith in the work of Yeshua.

So, because it's not dependent on how hard or long I pray for the miracle, or how hard I "work" for it, I don't need to worry about the results. The results are then no longer my responsibility. I don't need control, because I've died to give it to Him. He will have His way, and I desire no other. There is freedom in realising this, and if we try to have control or have things go our way in all situations, we are creating an incompatibility with the Holy Spirit within us. He is not really interested in our ways, or how what He is doing makes us feel. Sometimes He does weird things, like walking on water or turning water into wine.

Many fellowships of believers are deprived of the works of the Holy Spirit because of this. You will not see them pray for each other, perform miracles of healing, cast out demons, or do anything supernatural. Many consider the Holy Spirit as merely a giver of wisdom or a teacher. He is those things, but the oppression of spiritual gifts because it offends our carnal mind is demonic. In doing so, we keep the Father from working in our lives and the lives of others—and more importantly, from using us to reach the lives of others through the miraculous.

If you do not see these things in your fellowship, I encourage you to seek them with joy. They are real, and the Father is busy with a latter-rain outpouring of the Spirit like never before. We are the best wine saved for last. You do not need to look far to find the thousands of believers from diverse backgrounds waking up to this outpouring of the Spirit of God. When I started praying for the sick and baptising on the streets only around three years ago in 2014, I hadn't really heard of anyone else who did the same. Since then, an explosion of people has awakened to this reality.

Additionally, we need to understand that not seeking or walking out your gifting due to unbelief is lawless. For we know that sin is lawlessness (1 John 3:4), and anything that does not come from faith, but rather unbelief in God, is sin (Romans 14:23). If we truly love Yeshua, we need to always do our best to walk as He walked, even if it is uncertain, causes us to fear, or causes discomfort. Love is not always easy, comfortable, formal, or pretty, but it is what He calls us to do.

LIGHT IN THE DARK

Once we come into a greater knowledge of truth, we often feel betrayed by the mainstream church, or anyone who either consciously or unconsciously fed us lies. Or our hearts may break for them, and in sharing the truth with them, we experience severe rejection.

In both cases, most believers who come to the knowledge of God's Torah start living a "set-apart" lifestyle. The "holy" kind of set-apartness is commanded by scripture. The Father desires and instructs us to follow His instructions, which causes us to look severely different from the world. I've asked the Father many times why He chose to reveal such amazing revelation to me. So many others who love Him have not been as blessed as me in some areas; I'm sure you feel the same about some things. But I've come to realise that, instead of merely contemplating it, I can use it as the driver to be a light to the darkness.

All too often, we confuse the set-apart holiness the Father desires for us with separating ourselves from the world. We are instructed to have a brighter, set-apart (different) light to present to the world, but not to hide that light under a basket. Do you not know, dear brothers and sisters, that the Father of lights has given you a flame to ignite others with?

And he said to them, "Is a lamp brought in to be put under a basket, or under a bed, and not on a stand? For nothing is hidden except to be made manifest; nor is anything secret except to come to light." **(MARK 4:21-22)**

"You are the light of the world. A city set on a hill cannot be hidden. Nor do people light a lamp and put it under a basket, but on a stand, and it gives light to all in the house. In the same way, let your light shine before others, **so that they may see your good works and give glory to your Father who is in heaven.**" **(MATTHEW 5:14-16, EMPHASIS ADDED)**

This should not be a strange concept. The Pharisees continuously persecuted Yeshua for this teaching. While He never compromised, He understood that light always expels the darkness, and that the darkness cannot touch His Flame, and that Flame is the Holy Spirit of God. We read how Yeshua was a friend to the lawless, a deliverer of infirmity, and hope to the lost. It is impossible for us to walk as He walked if we excommunicate everyone we don't agree with, even if they are sinners (lawless).

Yeshua loved them into the arms of the Father through the empowerment of the Holy Spirit. Without the Spirit, we will be afraid; we won't love the lost or those in sin. The Holy Spirit gives discernment that our battle has never been against our brothers in sin, but against higher powers of darkness. He also enables us to see people through the lens of the Father and love them like He does. Often, we treat others within the identity the world has given them and expect them to change. Instead, we need to love them with the identity the Father declares over them, even if we aren't seeing them walk in it yet, so that they might understand and step into it. Treat others with the same identity as the identity that the Father gives you—a child of the living God.

This love should extend not only to the sinner, but also to the widow and the orphan. We may give a donation here and there to make ourselves feel better inside, but the Father calls a radical generation to care for the widows, the orphans, and the poor. The reason for this is not only to display to the world what the true love of God looks like, but also to teach us His love in the process. We complain how we don't have the love to give, but fail to realise that it is by the act of giving that the love manifests. Going against our flesh, which doesn't want to love, and loving someone unconditionally who doesn't deserve it often changes our heart even more than it changes the person we minister to.

This has changed my life. Instead of waiting for the love to come, stepping out and loving in action against my fleshly desires sparked the flame of God's love within me for my neighbour. When we shema (listen and obey), the Spirit follows the Word and changes our hearts to fulfil it. It has become way too easy to tithe to a ministry, expecting others to do the hard lifting, while we remain passive towards the lost and needy in our fellowships. It is demonic, and we will need to give an account.

My encounter at Hatfield Square that night wasn't what changed my life. It was the continuous pursuit of more of Him that did. From that point on, I started going out both alone and with outreach groups on a weekly basis for years to come, with the heart of reaching the lost. I've gone into some of the most dangerously violent places with the heart of spreading the gospel. I say this not to boast, but to demonstrate the following: the Holy Spirit receives all glory for that boldness, empowerment, and destruction of fear within me. It is by ministering to the sinner, the lawless, that the love of the Holy Spirit physically moves through us to reach the person.

I thought I had some good measure of love before all this, but I had no idea. I started weeping for the lost in late nights of prayer, where the broken didn't leave my mind. Many believers never experience this, only because they are not walking out this part of Yeshua. We can obey Truth and keep the Sabbath as much as we want, but if we don't walk in the things of the Spirit and minister to the lost like Yeshua did, we have a half-baked walk and are just picking-and-choosing the part of Yeshua we want. I say this in such love: God longs for a generation that will not walk in only Spirit or only Truth, but in the full revelation and reality of both. It is attainable.

Many have told me that I'm called to be an evangelist and "that is why this is your heart." I have come to realise my primary calling is not an evangelist, but rather a teacher. Furthermore, we are all called to evangelism, for it was a large part of Yeshua's walk. You cannot claim to walk like Yeshua yet not physically love on people in this life. Unfortunately, our modern culture has settled for Facebook debates as the new evangelism, while the desperate poor man on the streets hungers and thirsts for righteousness.

Please, don't take my word for it. Go out onto the streets and see for yourself. People are starving. This past weekend we went on an outreach and, while my friend was preaching, a man came to the side with his mouth wide open while he listened to the gospel. He cried at the sight of receiving a Bible. If this does not become part of your lifestyle, you will never develop the love for people the Messiah instructs us to have.

This love doesn't come by merely studying the Word, but by walking the Word out in action.

Let our statements of, "Here I am, send them!" turn into "Here I am, Father, send me."

INTRODUCTION TO THE GIFTS
Goal of the gifts and how they work

Faith is the requirement and activator for the Holy Spirit to move, but the Holy Spirit is also not contained by it. When a miracle takes place through the Spirit, it is often a pure manifestation of God's grace that can happen even in the presence of unbelief. However, this is the exception and not the norm—God is sovereign and can do as He desires, but He prefers to move through those who follow the perfect example of Yeshua.

So, what do we see in Yeshua? As discussed before, we see a great walk of obedience and fear of God that continues in the holiness that God declared over Him. We also see a great manifestation of spiritual gifts and works of the Spirit, more than any book can contain. We cannot deny that spiritual gifts were an integral part of Yeshua's ministry. Without the miracles, signs, and wonders, He would not have been able to fulfil the fullness of His calling. I would like to submit to you that the same is true for us. There is One Spirit that distributes gifts to each believer as he desires (1 Corinthians 12:11). But I do not want you to be ignorant regarding this, as many are under the impression that they will simply wake up one day with the gift of healing, tongues, or miracles:

You do not have, because you do not ask. **(JAMES 4:2)**

"If you then, being wicked, know how to give good gifts to your children, how much more shall your Father who is in the heavens give what is good to those who ask Him!"
(MATTHEW 7:11)

The reality is that God desires us to make our needs known to Him, even though He knows them before we ask. You will not receive a spiritual gift from God without sincerely desiring and making your request known at the Throne of God. I have found that, in the same way that people use excuses for why they are not "ready" for baptism yet, we make excuses for why we are not "ready" for the gift yet. It is interesting that we equate our apparent lack of holiness and works to being unworthy of the Holy Spirit or the gifts He distributes.

If we want to work for receiving Him, we will never satisfy the standard. We will never be good enough per our works for the fullness of God to indwell us. And if He chose to work through vessels only as perfect as Yeshua, no man will see Him work through him ever, for we have all fallen short of the glory of God (Romans 3:23).

Because we have received the Holy Spirit by faith and not works, we also receive the gifts He distributes by faith and not works. This is very important to understand and believe, because if you receive the gift of healing and are driven by an approved-by-works mindset, you will not see healing manifest in the way and as frequently as He desires. You will not be able to see healing (or any gift) flow if you don't have a clean conscience. Yeshua died for you to have a clean conscience before the Father (Hebrews 10:22), to enter His presence with freedom, and work from (instead of to) the Throne of God with freedom. This means that the sins we all have, but repent from, will not affect our results. It can only affect our results if we allow the enemy to convince us that God will not heal this person because we weren't perfect today.

I will touch on a few spiritual gifts in this book, but before I do, we need to understand what they were given for. The spiritual gifts have two purposes: First, to **empower** and **edify** the Body of Christ. Second, as a **sign** and **witness** to the world of the testimony of Yeshua.

SPIRITUAL GIFTS: A SIGN TO THE LOST

Much of the Truth Group has a great understanding of truth, but lacks the power to communicate it.

And my speech and my preaching was not with enticing words of man's wisdom, but in demonstration of the Spirit and of power. **(1 CORINTHIANS 2:4)**

Paul is an excellent example. He was the "Pharisee of Pharisees," the most zealous of all; a scholar of the Scriptures, and a student of the highly-respected Gamliel (Philippians 3:5). In all his wisdom of the Word, he was most dependent on the "demonstration of the Spirit and power." If the spiritual gifts of power were a necessity to him, why do we think we can complete our ministerial callings without them? We truly take away from the gift of Truth the Father has given us by abandoning His Spirit that empowers Truth.

As previously discussed, we also see in the ministry of Yeshua that spiritual gifts were a primary driver. The Spirit and its wonders were a witness of the Truth within Yeshua, as well as a witness of God's love, kindness, and grace to the lost. When the Father prescribes curses for transgressing His Torah (Deuteronomy 28), then comes in the flesh to heal the infirmities and reverse the curses of the transgressors, it truly is a marvellous display of His grace. After praying for them, He instructed them to repent immediately, lest something worse come upon them (John 5:14).

The kindness of God is what leads people to repentance. After Jesus manifests a miracle that nobody deserves, somebody comes to repentance. The law shows us what sin is, but sometimes people need to witness the holiness of God to see the lawlessness within themselves. When we pray for them, even though they don't deserve it, the manifestation of His holiness provides a contrast to demonstrate the lawlessness of the sinner. This physical "manifestation of holiness" cannot take place in and through us without our intimate relationship with the Holy Spirit.

On a street outreach one time, I prayed for a man on the streets who was drawn to the hot food we were making. Josh didn't know Yeshua, and when he found out I follow Yeshua, he wanted to argue with the Scriptures on how Yeshua was not the Messiah. I knew this debate-driven conversation would be fruitless, so I immediately laid hands on him and prayed for him. I prayed for the Father to come and reveal to Josh the truth, and I prayed for a baptism of the Holy Spirit.

After "amen," Josh looked at me and said, "The pain in my chest ran away. I felt something come from the left side of my body and go right through me." I explained to Josh the Holy Spirit sent by Yeshua when He ascended, and the debate was over. (This encounter was caught on video, and is viewable on the Rise on Fire YouTube Channel. Video Title: "Saving the Streets - Miracle Outreach.")

IDENTITY WITHOUT REPENTANCE

This world needs the view of the true grace of God, not the lawless, hyper-grace teaching of many western churches that teach identity without repentance. You can teach someone who they are in Yeshua (identity), and they might be able to do mighty miracles through that, but if they do not understand repentance and obedience, they are on the highway to hell paved with good intentions. Without true repentance (confessing and turning from sin), there is no forgiveness. By this it is incredibly important to follow the model of evangelism proven by Yeshua. After praying for someone and witnessing God do a miracle for them to demonstrate His kindness, we need to swiftly bring them the "hard to swallow" news: they need Yeshua, need to repent, be baptized, and die to themselves so they can rise with Him unto a new creation.

Unless we preach the Truth to follow the miracle, even though we give God the glory, we become endorsers of lawlessness without even realising it. Many from the Grace Group have grown content with preaching His love and grace without preaching the coming judgement of God that no one can escape. I urge you to walk in the fullness of the Spirit and preach repentance. If you do this, the Spirit will confirm this Word by greater signs and wonders than ever thought possible to many.

SPIRITUAL GIFTS: EDIFYING THE BODY OF CHRIST

In addition to spiritual gifts witnessing about the Truth as a sign to the lost, the Father has also given them to edify the body of believers. The lack of understanding and "walking out" of the spiritual gifts provided by the Holy Spirit has caused a great lack of fruit in some Torah (Truth Group) fellowships around the world. Generally speaking, some of these groups of fellowship rarely pray for one another—and by "praying for one another," I mean literally laying hands on each other and bringing the needs of brothers and sisters before the Father. Our sick brothers and sisters leave sick; we do not receive encouragement through personal prophecy; we struggle with the discernment of spirits; we don't deal with demons, etc.

Brothers and sisters, I was once there. I was frustrated that I did not see these things anywhere except in the Scriptures. But radically seeking it from the Father yielded great results. What father would give his son a stone when he asks for bread? (Matthew 7:11)

Simply allowing the existing deep-rooted desires in our hearts to take ground and bear good fruit will change our fellowships forever. During my life, I have been in a diverse collection of fellowships, from Spirit-focussed fellowships—where the miraculous becomes the norm but the Truth is not always welcome—to the Truth-focussed fellowships—where the Truth has the final say as long as the Spirit does not push us out of our comfort zones. I believe the Father has brought me through these diverse places to teach me their strengths and weaknesses. Today I proclaim to you that we cannot afford to quench the workings of the Spirit within the Body of Christ. It would be like taking oil out of an engine—a lot of noise followed by smoke.

The spiritual gifts within the fellowship also mature the love of God in and through us for our brothers and sisters in the faith. In my life, the spiritual gifts were one of the main contributors to developing my love for people—both the saved and the unsaved. Because when they manifest, I become the channel for the river to flow through. I might not always be able to control the river, for the river flows where and how He wishes.

According to 1 Corinthians 14, these are some of the spiritual gifts:

- Healing
- Tongues
- Interpretation of Tongues
- Gift of Miracles/Wonders
- Word of Wisdom

- *Word of Knowledge*
- *Discerning of Spirits*
- *Gift of Faith/Belief*
- *Prophecy*

I encourage you to go down this list and search your heart for the desire you have, which the Father has already given you, towards any one of the gifts, and ask. We have not because we **ask** not. In my asking, the Father (by His grace) has allowed me to see each one I've asked for. The Spirit of God wants to use us to reach both the saved and unsaved. Don't let the enemy convince you that you are unworthy, unready, or not ordained. Yeshua died, was raised, and ascended to send us His Spirit, to enable His children to walk in the fullness of Him, to crush the Kingdom of darkness alongside Him, to set the captives free and see the lame walk.

In the following pages, I will be going through some of the spiritual gifts the Holy Spirit has been gracious enough to use me in. You will not find a "How to Heal People 101" in the Scriptures, nor in this book, because the Holy Spirit is the giver and teacher of the gifts. The Father wants us to learn the gifts through practical experience. That means stepping out of your comfort zone, being bold and proclaiming freedom even if you are afraid or feel your belief is shaky. In the beginning, His grace is sufficient, and you will see great results despite your unbelief if you are steadfast and trustworthy in continuing to seek the gift despite any failures, unsatisfactory results, or what you perceive by sight. If you don't let what you see discourage you from what the Word says you're supposed to see, the Spirit will count you a worthy steward of the gift and the results we see in Scripture will become a reality.

A lot of people have a misconception that a gift is something that just "lands on us" in a burning bush moment. I don't discount that possibility, but the reality for most of the disciples was that they dwelled with Him and started practically stepping out and "trained" for it. Just like anything in life, practices makes perfect—the gifts are the same. The Father provides the desire—the wood to get the fire started—but we need to learn how to light that fire within ourselves. We can then start walking in a place where the fire is consistently lit, from the fellowship, to the street, to the workplace. It's simple: the more you exercise that spiritual muscle, the more powerful the muscle becomes to push and influence the spiritual realm.

BELIEVING IN THE FATHER'S WILL & BELIEVING OUR AUTHORITY

If we try to play a game without understanding the rules, or if we doubt our own ability to play the game, we will really struggle. Similarly, if you try to give a word of knowledge, or see the sick recover, yet doubt His will or even yourself, you have lost the battle before even beginning.

Many excuses have formed inside the church organisations and groups of fellowship for why we don't see what Scripture states we are supposed to see. One of these excuses has been that "it is not His will to heal you." Unless the Father has come in a burning bush moment to tell us this, we cannot make such a statement. In many cases it is of demonic origin. One of the biggest reasons for a passive body of Christ is the doubt in God's will. If I pray for blind eyes to open but question whether He wants them to open, then I have lost already.

God does have a sovereign will, but it is not for us to dictate that will. In scripture, every single sick or lame person who came to Yeshua left healed. He never made an excuse covered by the will of His Father. He was the walking image of the invisible God (Colossians 1:15), and He is the perfect example for us to follow. If He never made excuses, why should we even think to do such a thing?

The thief cometh not, but for to steal, and to kill, and to destroy: I am come that they might have life, and that they might have it more abundantly. **(JOHN 10:10)**

In my approach of always seeing someone through God's eyes, with every ailment as an opportunity for God's will of healing, deliverance, and freedom to manifest, it was a game changer. I have taken out many brothers and sisters in discipleship to teach them how to walk in this. The usual prayer taught by churches is, "If it is Your will, heal her." There is nothing wrong with this prayer in itself, for we should always follow His will. But, most of the time, this prayer is not prayed from a heart of humility, but rather unbelief.

By saying in our prayer that it is dependent on God's will, it somehow provides us with a means of escape when it doesn't happen. It is a cowardly prayer of unbelief that never sees healing come. A simple shift to believing that it is God's will to heal everyone that comes to you, just like Yeshua walked it out, changes everything. Now the prayer doesn't question God's will anymore, but declares His will. If we are called to be a light to the world, yet do not believe it is His will to destroy the works of the devil, how can we declare something we don't 100% believe in?

"If it is Your will, heal her."
"Sickness, I command you right now, come out of Him—pain, leave right now!"

See the difference? Now we are not asking a demon or sickness to leave, we are commanding it to. The Father didn't tell us to question His will to heal the sick; He commanded us to simply "heal the sick" (Matthew 10:8).

And straightway the father of the child cried out, and said with tears, Lord, I believe; help **thou mine unbelief**. When Jesus saw that the people came running together, he rebuked the foul spirit, saying unto him, **Thou dumb and deaf spirit, I charge thee, come out of him, and enter no more into him**. **(MARK 9:24-25, EMPHASIS ADDED)**

Yeshua could have prayed, "Father, if it is your will for this sickness to leave, please let him go." But He never did. In His demonstration to us as His disciples, we receive a clear picture and understanding on how to pray in authority.

When discipling others, I've seen them pray for someone incorrectly. But when I gave the simple instruction to pray in greater authority by commanding things to happen, the healing instantly came—ministered by the same person who had no success only moments ago.

It's not about a prayer; it's not about the words; it's about what lies behind them. We just happen to connect unbelief to some words and authority to others in our English language.

MIRACLES WITHOUT PRAYER

Some time ago, after ministering with friends at a local shopping centre, the Father permitted me to demonstrate something to them.

As we were getting in our car to leave, we saw a man walking with an injured leg. As my friends called him, I told him from about 10-15 meters away to stop and stand still right there. I pointed to him with my finger and just smiled. Inside, I didn't pray anything or think anything; I just rested and waited a few seconds for the Spirit to do His thing. After about 10 seconds, I told the man to move his leg around and test it out. He was instantly and completely healed on the spot and walked up to us perfectly. Everyone was blown away, because we just realised that it's not about following a specific prayer formula, but simple belief.

Sometimes the belief issue we have is not that He cannot do it, but rather that He won't or cannot do it through us. We have all kinds of reasons for believing this—whether the enemy has convinced us that we have "too much sin," or that we don't "have the gift," or whatever.

Today I would like to tell you that reading this book demonstrates that you have already been chosen to walk in power for His glory. We need to stop listening to lies that cloud our belief in Him and in ourselves. We need to believe in ourselves too, that we can accomplish remarkable things for the Kingdom of God, not because of what we've done, but because of what He says and has done. I am not talking about self-worship, but rather the issue of low self-esteem. It is sin, because low self-esteem comes from not believing what God's Word says about you:

Fear not, for I am with you; be not dismayed, for I am your God; I will strengthen you, I will help you, I will uphold you with my righteous right hand. **(ISAIAH 41:10)**

So that Christ may dwell in your hearts through faith—that you, being rooted and grounded in love, may have strength to comprehend with all the saints what is the breadth and length and height and depth, and to know the love of Christ that surpasses knowledge, that you may be filled with all the **fullness of God**. **(EPHESIANS 3:17-19, EMPHASIS ADDED)**

Because you are **precious** in my eyes, and **honored**, and **I love you, I give men** in return for you, peoples in exchange for your life. **Fear not**, for **I am with you**; I will bring your offspring from the east, and from the west I will gather you. **(ISAIAH 43:4-5, EMPHASIS ADDED)**

But you are a **chosen** race, a **royal** priesthood, a **holy** nation, a people for his own possession, that you may proclaim the excellencies of him who called you out of darkness into his marvelous **light**. **(1 PETER 2:9, EMPHASIS ADDED)**

For I know the plans I have for you, declares the Lord, plans for welfare and not for evil, to give you a future and a hope. **(JEREMIAH 29:11, EMPHASIS ADDED)**

Often men attach *ifs* to many things, including our acceptance by them. We are accepted by men only when we tell them what they want to hear, or do what they want to see. God, however, declares and restores a new identity unto us as soon as we choose Him. He loves you, declares you royal and holy, and even honours you—not because of what you've done, but because of who you are: a child of the living God. And if the Father of the universe is your Abba, why do you fear what someone thinks? All that now matters is what He says and thinks. For one day, we will all stand before Him. All voices will go quiet with the wave of His hand—He will speak, and those voices will never be raised against you again. Please understand and believe this, for it will determine how you live your life unto death, and therefore how you are judged on Judgement Day.

HEALING THE SICK

After my encounter at Hatfield square, I woke up the next morning and knew nothing would ever be the same again. Every sick person I walked by or encountered in my daily walk turned from a challenge into an opportunity. I genuinely started feeling incredibly excited when I saw sick people!

I mean, it wasn't that I wanted them sick, but I saw sickness as an opportunity for the Kingdom of God to manifest. In the first week after my encounter, I was telling my friends at university of what happened. As I was ending my testimony, two atheists from our department of study walked out of the entrance right past us to go sit on a bench. My friends took a long stare at the one atheist who was walking cripple with her leg in a cast, then gave me "the stare," hinting something obvious. I'll be honest, I was a little nervous. But I knew what I experienced was true, and I was reminded of the nights I begged God for His Spirit. Did He give me the biggest gift (Holy Spirit) ever, just to keep it to myself? As my friends watched, I prayed a quick prayer to the Father and walked over to the two atheists sitting on the bench. I had never met them before, so I introduced myself and asked the girl with the cast if she had pain.

"Yeah, I do when I put pressure on it," she said. "Why?" I told her that I'd like to pray for her, that I believe Jesus will take all her pain right now. Sitting on the bench—all laid back and with a cigarette in her mouth—she checks me out top to bottom, sighs, and says, "O.K." I placed my hand on her leg and prayed, "Father, I thank you so much. We command all this pain to leave her leg right now. I thank you for complete restoration, Amen."

After I prayed, I told her to stand up and put pressure on her leg. When she stood up and very sceptically applied pressure to her leg, she looked at me with enlarged eyes and said, "It's better!" Her friend next to her jumped up and said, "Are you serious!?"

She still had a little bit of pain left when applying a lot of pressure. After one more prayer, she grabbed her friend's hand and started to walk away. When she awkwardly thanked me, and I simply responded, "It's all Jesus. He loves you!" In a matter of seconds, her entire belief system taught by the world came crashing down; and it was way too overwhelming for the moment—they had no idea how to react.

As I looked at them walking off (with her no longer walking cripple), I realised the impact and power of the Holy Spirit. No debate was necessary. I didn't require wise words or eloquent speech, but only the demonstration of the Spirit:

And my speech and my preaching was not with enticing words of man's wisdom, but in demonstration of the Spirit and of power. **(1 CORINTHIANS 2:4)**

Paul, as well as I, isn't against Godly words of wisdom—they do have a place. But many people, just like me in my past, spent so much time growing in the knowledge of God through His Word only to weaken it by not empowering the Truth by the Spirit of God. Many men far more noble than me have spent their entire lives devoted to spreading the Good News, but with a false belief that the Spirit no longer does the things in the Way He used to. This belief (or rather unbelief) prevents the Spirit from moving in power the way we see in the life of Yeshua. I am not talking down on my Godly brothers and sisters who walk in Truth and preach the gospel in a different way. But according to the example of Yeshua, if we are not walking in the fullness of Spirit and Truth, we will see only half the fruit.

If we choose to follow a doctrine of man instead of the pure and simple example of Christ—because we are "grown up" and theological, instead of children—we will be held accountable by the Father. Furthermore, if we allow what we see around us in the lives of others to determine what we should see, we are setting ourselves up for the same failure. The number one reason we pray for the sick should not be to see them healed, but because He commanded us to:

Heal the sick, cleanse the lepers, raise the dead, cast out devils: freely ye have received, freely give. **(MATTHEW 10:8)**

If any doctrine or teaching, no matter who teaches it or how many believe it, teaches that we should not walk exactly as He walked, then that is **false doctrine**. He is the perfect walking example for us to follow. God came in the flesh to provide us with this example, to provide a simple means of walking as He walked. By doing this, He eradicated all possible excuses we have left for unrighteousness (disobedience to Truth) or unbelief (disobedience to Spirit). There are truly no more excuses left, and telling the Father on Judgement Day that "no one else showed me" would be ridiculous, for He already showed you. We are not called to follow men or seminary, but the example of Yeshua. It's the simplicity of the gospel, and anything else is pure demonic.

We have such a love for Yeshua and following the Truth and holiness, but we miss the biggest element that makes it possible to communicate it to a lost and dying world. Yeshua chose fishermen for a reason, to demonstrate that He often even prefers to use the weak and least—those who didn't go to seminary or have good "manners." This demonstrates that preaching the gospel was never meant to be left to your pastor or church elders; the responsibility is all on you. By the empowerment of the Holy Spirit, and understanding the fundamental Truth, anyone can preach the gospel to the lost—and everyone should. Because we have traded the Spirit of God for the wisdom of men, we are left just as powerless and broken as this world. We have the Truth but not the fruit; we have the Truth, but not the Power that was designed to follow it.

In my discovery of Truth in my earlier years, many of my friends didn't understand me. I had a "weird belief" that sounded different from the mainstream. I hotly debated some of them in trying to convince them of what the Father has revealed to me, but it seemed to yield no real fruit. Years later, after I was changed by the Spirit that night at Hatfield Square, many of my friends who previously discounted my revelations came to me once again, and their curiosity turned into an actual understanding of what I was preaching in the first place: the Truth. But what changed?

The love, the fruit, the power—they wanted it. They had seen some of this in their churches before, but because a greater measure of Truth accompanied the Spirit within me, a greater measure of power, love, and fruit followed. The Spirit has always been the witness to the Truth, to convict the world of sin (lawlessness), righteousness, and judgement (John 16:8). If the person does not preach against lawlessness, but rather that the law is abolished, the Spirit will not follow with the same measure of power.

In fact, the Holy Spirit was so alive with the Truth within me that I started seeing incurable diseases like cancer, blindness, HIV/Aids and others leave after having only a few months of experience praying for the sick. The primary reason for this is not only that the Spirit follows Truth, but also that within me was a faith grown by obedience years in advance.

FAITH COMES THROUGH TRUTH

So also faith by itself, if it does not have works, is dead. But someone will say, "You have faith and I have works." Show me your faith apart from your works, and I will show you my faith by my works. You believe that God is one; you do well. Even the demons believe—and shudder! Do you want to be shown, you foolish person, that faith apart from works is useless? **(JAMES 2:17-20)**

While we are saved by faith and not works, after our salvation, works becomes the evidence of our faith. Faith and works cannot be disconnected, for they live in unity. Faith without works is dead. By works, we are referring to obedience of God's instructions. What most fail to realise is that God designed His instructions to grow our faith among other things. The Israelites failed to obey God when He instructed them to not collect the manna on the seventh day Sabbath (Exodus 16:26), but through their disobedience suffered the consequences of having no manna (food) to collect on the seventh day anyway. The root issue of this disobedience wasn't just pure rebellion, but rather unbelief. They simply did not believe that God would provide enough manna for them on the six days to last them for the seventh day Sabbath. After that incident, the Israelites quickly learned to trust in God by resting from their labour on the Sabbath day.

This is amazing, because we learn that the Sabbath was teaching belief to the children of Israel! At the time when I started walking in the power of the Holy Spirit, I had been keeping the Sabbath for five years! I would like to testify to you firsthand that the fourth commandment of keeping the Sabbath was a primary driver in developing my faith for enabling great works of the Holy Spirit in and through me. This is not even considering all the other commandments I kept that contributed even further.

We need to understand that, while we do not receive the Holy Spirit by works (Galatians 3:2), works of obedience builds our faith and belief necessary to walk in the fullness of the Holy Spirit. Where unbelief is, or where our flesh is empowered through lawlessness, the Holy Spirit cannot go. Where belief is, and where our Spirit is empowered through obedience, the Holy Spirit goes (Romans 8:6-7).

This is only a small part of how Spirit strengthens Truth and Truth strengthens Spirit.

THE RACE OF RESULTS

After the Father's miracle in Hatfield Square, He did something unusual. By His grace, I saw 100% results for the next month. Everyone I prayed for got healed. But soon I realised He wanted to teach me something more than seeing the results.

After around a month, I was asked to pray for a lame man. As I laid hands on him, prayed, and lifted my hands, he didn't get healed. I prayed again, and again, for about an hour.

I left there distraught. After seeing complete success for a month, it seemed like it would be this way the rest of my life. This caused me to come crashing down hard. I would like to clarify that this part of the story is unusual. Most people do not see the "success rates" I saw in the very beginning; instead it is usually a gradual increase as we grow.

But the Father wanted to teach me something: I had been chasing results. Without realising, I started to become driven by the results—the amount and size of the miracle. Chasing after miracles seems like an obvious thing to stay away from, but it is something everyone will struggle with at one point or another.

If the primary reason you pray for someone is to see a miracle, you are deceived. We don't pray because we want to see a miracle; we pray because that's who we are. We pray because He instructed us to simply "lay your hands on the sick." He has declared an identity of authority over sickness to us and commanded us to cleanse the leper and cast out demons (Matthew 10:8). We do it because we love Him and want to be obedient. Now, from this perspective, the results aren't even in the picture. They have rather become the "cherry on the cake."

If you live by results, you will fall by results, and that is what it felt like when I prayed and he didn't get healed. Results can be inconsistent (more so in the beginning stages), and we cannot afford to live by such inconsistency. God, on the other hand, He never changes.

By adopting this mindset, you won't get discouraged if you don't see what you wanted to see, because you're not driven by that. You will actually start seeing more "cherries on the cake" (miracles) because, when you run after Him, that's exactly what you'll get. We have not been instructed to run a race of results, a race after miracles, after salvations, after perfection. These amazing elements are part of the race; they encourage us and build our faith, but they are not the goal. We have been called to run after Him—and when we seek first the Kingdom of God, the rest will be added unto us:

Do you not know that those who run in a race indeed all run, but one receives the prize? Run in such a way as to obtain it.
(1 CORINTHIANS 9:24)

Many also think that "heaven" is the prize. But for me, I just want Yeshua. Moses told the Father that if He wants to destroy the Israelites after building the golden calf, He needs to blot out the name of Moses from the book of life as well (Exodus 32:32). Moses was more concerned with restoring God's relationship with His people than his own eternity. In retrospect, anything else would be selfish. Moses doesn't deserve eternal life—none of them did—and he knew that. Do we share the heart of Moses to be willing to sacrifice a heavenly eternal inheritance for the sinners around us? We need to be so desperate for their salvation that we would be willing to die for them not only physically, but also eternally.

If we get our hearts to this place of sacrificial love for God's people, we will see the miracles of Moses and greater than these, for we have the fullness of Spirit and Truth.

CASTING OUT DEMONS

Alicia (not her real name) was an alcoholic seeking freedom. Standing in the middle of the room, everyone wanted to pray for her. Suddenly, her voiced deepened and she started convulsing, seemingly out of her own control. Everyone took a step back. I was the only one left in the foreground. I looked around, and everyone looked at me—the only one left.

I had never faced a demon like this before. I was scared, to be honest. But I'd been praying for many to get healed at this point. So, I tried my best: "I command you, in the name of Jesus, to come out right now!"

The demon said no, but I continued. After a few minutes, he weakened and weakened, until he left her completely. She did not remember much—it's like she was unconscious. But she felt free, although tired and weak.

In the following months, the Father arranged it so that I encountered demons on multiple occasions. Not much later, our ministry visited a church, preached the gospel, and baptised over 15 individuals after they came to repentance. At least 10 of them manifested demons as they hit the water. It was like the demons fell into fire, and they were cast out easily and within minutes.

When we left that night, we were in awe. We had never seen baptisms like that before, and I was questioning why. Why do we see churches baptize so many, yet never like this? I have come to learn that there are a few reasons.

Casting out demons is one of the most misunderstood and underutilized spiritual acts in the lives of believers. We have grown disobedient to the instruction of Yeshua to cast out demons, and have left it to the "deliverance ministries" or pastor. There are many lies surrounding demons, and the reason is obvious: demons lie. And they lie more about themselves than anything else. If the enemy can convince believers to preach that we don't need to deal with demons—that demons will "come after you" or that we need to fear them—then the enemy has won. He has made us passive and afraid, and he has yet again succeeded in selling us a counterfeit identity not of God, an identity that can't deal with demons.

In my first time facing the demon of alcoholism with Alicia, I was afraid. But I was afraid only because I was taught to be while growing up. We are conditioned not only by churches, but also horror movies and other demonic matters of the world that the kingdom of darkness is powerful, scary, and that it can even kill you.

This teaching is demonic, and we need to seriously start considering what we allow ourselves and our kids to watch. We are being programmed by the kingdom of darkness to believe that we cannot fight back. We have ended up with a generation of soldiers for God who have believed they are babies. Satan knows that when we understand we are powerful soldiers given great spiritual authority (identity), armour (defence) and a powerful weapon (Spirit and Truth) by the King, then he's done. But if he can convince us to believe otherwise, then God's army becomes paralyzed—they think they have nothing while, in reality, they are walking with a giant sword on their back.

This is exactly what has happened. Therefore, we don't see the average believer casting out demons left and right. Yes, this really is for every believer. Aside from the numerous occasions Yeshua, our perfect example, casted out demons, we see the apostles as well as 70 other disciples doing the same. These 70 disciples went from home to home to heal the sick, cast out demons, and fulfil the great commission (Luke 10:1-12).

Go! See, I send you out as lambs into the midst of wolves.
(LUKE 10:3)

Appointing such a large group of believers to face the enemy head-on alone may seem "irresponsible" of Yeshua to do. Indeed, He tells them that they are sent as "lambs into the midst of wolves." The most important thing taught to all His followers was to fear God, for in fearing God, we give God authority. If, however, we fear the enemy and his demons, we give them authority, for fear of the enemy is rooted in our unbelief that God remains unchallenged.

If you have this unbelief and fear of Satan, you give him authority to attack you. While dealing with casting out demons for years now, I have never received any amount of attack that is noteworthy. It has been nothing more than mere irritations. Some others have had different experiences and more severe attacks, but it is because they fear demons, thereby giving them free reign and access to attack as they wish. But a mere peasant will not attack a king who knows his identity as a king, and the authority that comes with that identity. By simply resting in my identity as a son with the fullness of God's Kingdom power behind me, I can rest in that and command the demonic to get behind me. When we know who we are through Yeshua, they will tremble at our voices.

Brothers and sisters, we are in a war, whether you want to be in one or not. You signed up for this when you signed up for Him. It is not a burden or something to be afraid of; it is the opportunity to fight right alongside Yeshua Himself.

You might be surprised when you understand that I'm being literal. He sent a Holy Spirit after He ascended. He said that it is a good thing, but how? The disciples were confused by this, but know today that it is a good thing because, through the Holy Spirit poured out on you, God accommodates and fights alongside you in every spiritual battle. This battle is against principalities of the kingdom of darkness, and it is driven by faith. You can come to a place where the unseen, spiritual realm of light and darkness can become more of a reality than the physical realm to us. When this happens, our faith starts looking like that of Yeshua and His disciples. They had great faith because they lived in a way that bled the spiritual realm right into the physical realm—so much so that it was just as easy to believe and have faith in the spiritual realm as it was to have faith in the physical realm.

This extends not only to dealing with demons, but healing too. Praying and believing for healing was much more difficult in the beginning than it is now. It has become such a normal thing for me—a part of this physical realm—that it is much easier to believe. This is one way in which our faith grows, through experience of the spiritual realm itself. Therefore, watching TV or going about your normal day-to-day life without engaging in spiritual activities will do nothing to grow your faith; it will merely grow the dominion of your flesh over you.

And these signs shall follow them that believe; In my name shall they cast out devils; they shall speak with new tongues; They shall take up serpents; and if they drink any deadly thing, it shall not hurt them; they shall lay hands on the sick, and they shall recover. So then after the Lord had spoken unto them, he was received up into heaven, and sat on the right hand of God. **(MARK 16:17-19)**

Why did Yeshua so specifically instruct us to "cast out demons"? He could have instructed many other important things in His last words before ascension. Casting out demons is one of the most important things we can do in our spiritual walk, because it's the closest we can get to facing the enemy head on.

Many other gifts glorify the Kingdom of God by destroying the works of the enemy, but casting out demons glorifies the Kingdom of God by destroying the enemy itself. Because we face the enemy head on while casting out demons, the spiritual realm is exposed to us in a way no other practical Kingdom application offers. This not only wakes us up to the reality of the realm, but also develops more faith within us to face it. It's one thing to say that we believe in a spiritual realm, but it's another thing to experience it and battle it head on alongside Yeshua.

After I started praying for healing, I was convinced that I believed the reality of the spiritual realm, but it was only after a certain demonic encounter on a video chat that I realised the depth of this.

Paul (not his real name) contacted me as a new believer. He believed he had been struggling with demons all his life, especially given his past with witchcraft. He lives overseas, so we made a video chat appointment. After some time talking, I started praying for him. "Every evil spirit of witchcraft, I command you, come out of him right now!"

Immediately Paul started making abnormal movements with his head, and he started to make groaning noises. After a few minutes of back-and-forth, I realised this demon was more stubborn than usual. God dropped it in my spirit to do something I've never done before. I told the demon, "I command you right now, look at Yeshua!"

His eyes enlarged and immediately locked on to the corner of the room while turning his head away. From his facial expression, it seemed like he was looking into a sun. He screamed, "No! It burns me!" and looked away. I commanded him again and his eyes locked on again as if he was forced. He had to obey! He started crying like a baby. I prayed to Yeshua and asked him to instruct the demon on what to do next.

A few seconds later, the demon called out, "I don't want to go to the pit!" I was shocked. I had never spoken of "the pit," but I immediately realised what was happening—Yeshua was there, and conversing with this evil spirit. In fear and anguish, the demon begged for mercy. In the beginning of the encounter, the demon was puffed up and proud, stating that he was a "legion" and that there were "many of them." He did all this to merely invoke a fear and unbelief in me. I did not listen or let it phase me, but continued. Why would I trust what a demon has to say?

In the later stages, after I told him to "look at Yeshua," he started becoming more and more like a baby character. Without over exaggeration, the demon started acting with the intelligence and personality of a baby while in the body of an adult man. The "big" demon that called himself legion was now turning into a baby that couldn't do anything else but cry for help. But how did this happen? It was not because of me, but because of what He has done and the authority given me (and all who believe in Yeshua), and because I believed it. It was not based on my holiness, performance, but merely believing that He has given me the same authority over the forces of darkness.

Understanding who I was, and walking that authority out in action by commanding the demon, caused the demon to become terrified. The demon is terrified of a son of God who understands who he is. A king who doesn't know his kingdom inheritance will not only be taken advantage of, but will also even pass his entire inheritance by. He does not understand his kingship authority and, because of that, others will not treat him in his royal identity. A son of God with a son of God's identity, while not believing or understanding that identity, will not cause any demon to submit or fear. If you cannot believe in the authority given to you by Yeshua, why would the enemy?

They know who we are; they know our relationship with God, whether we are warriors for God or passive, lukewarm professors of faith. They also know whether we know who we are, and when we do, it terrifies them. They might not show it to you, because it will not profit them; they will initially still try to fool you into believing the counterfeit identity that the enemy sold Adam and Eve in the garden—which was not the identity of power and authority God gave. They will try to fool you by lying and telling you how big they are and how insignificant you are, but once you start raising your authoritative voice against them, backed by the Kingdom of God, they will soon become as terrified as babies.

By the end of the session, while the demon was in this "crying baby state," he said, "You are destroying our kingdom!" The show was over; the demon was destroyed; he knew he was about to leave, and he was waving the white flag. Don't you want this? Don't you want demons begging at your feet and leaving at your call, as they obeyed Yeshua? We should want that, because it's part of the great commission.

The Father is calling out His bride to walk in this authority. If you do not prepare for the storm now, but rather opt to be an observer instead of a partaker, you will not stand a chance once the tribulation hits. If we cannot cast out the demons of this age, how will we stand against the forces of darkness that will be unleashed at the end of the age?

And he opened the bottomless pit; and there arose a smoke out of the pit, as the smoke of a great furnace; and the sun and the air were darkened by reason of the smoke of the pit. And there came out of the smoke locusts upon the earth: and unto them was given power, as the scorpions of the earth have power. **(REVELATION 9:2)**

I share this not as a means of scaring you, but as a means of waking you to the truth. This is merely the training ground for what is to come. Get trained up, for we are heading for D-Day. Most believers in the Truth Group are not ready for this. They do not have the faith that comes through practical application (walking it out) because they have been busier with knowledge than application. It is time.

God wants to do this alongside us. When we meet Him in our secret places of intimacy behind closed doors, He will show up at the battle alongside us—because He knows us and we know Him. When we call on His name, He answers, He delivers, He brings freedom. For where the Spirit of God is, there is deliverance (2 Corinthians 3:17). So why do you wait? Rise and pick up your weapons; it's time for battle. Those weapons were bought for a high price by the life of God. He wants us to use them to destroy the kingdom of darkness.

The demon left, and Paul did not remember much of what had happened except for mere flashes of memory here and there. After telling him, we cried together, for he said he felt incredibly free. This was a feeling he was not familiar with. Since a young age, the witchcraft in his family had taken hold of him ... until that day. There are many believers who walk around like Paul, ineffective for the kingdom, and they seem to walk in constant oppression even though they are saved. They are being oppressed by the demonic, and it is our responsibility to cast them out— to set people free and tell them to repent, be baptized, and filled with the Holy Spirit who will empower them to do the same.

But how do we fight demons if we never encounter them? We don't encounter demons because we don't want to. We need to ask God to use us against the kingdom of darkness as a soldier.

The Torah states that, when Israel entered battle, the commanders had to walk up and down the lines and tell the scared men to go back home, lest they cause the other soldiers to doubt in the power of God:

And the officers shall speak further unto the people, and they shall say, 'What man is there that is fearful and fainthearted? let him go and return unto his house, lest his brethren's heart faint as well as his heart.
(DEUTERONOMY 20:8)

It will be the same for this current and coming spiritual war.

The Commander will not put you on the front lines if you are a coward. You need to walk up to the Commander and tell Him, "Here I am, Lord. Send me to the lost, waste places and kingdoms of darkness. Put me on the front lines to fight alongside You. Let us destroy the enemy."

Strengthen the weak hands, and make firm the weak knees. **(ISAIAH 35:3)**

The Father will honour your prayer and place you in a place of training when you are ready for it. And in the end, He will use only His trained and best for the coming end-time battle on the front lines. Many of the rest will not survive.

In the battles of this world, those on the front lines usually die first, but in the battles of God's Kingdom, being with Him is where you survive, for he is a King who battles on the frontlines.

And the spirit cried, and rent him sore, and came out of him: and he was as one dead; insomuch that many said, He is dead. But Jesus took him by the hand, and lifted him up; and he arose. And when he was come into the house, his disciples asked him privately, 'Why could not we cast him out? And he said unto them, This kind can come forth by nothing, **but by prayer and fasting. (MARK 9:26-28, EMPHASIS ADDED)**

Yeshua cast out the demon that the disciples struggled to cast out earlier that day. In Matthew's account of the story (Matthew 17:20), He told them they failed because of their unbelief. The solution He provides to cure their unbelief is prayer and fasting (Mark 9:28).

Prayer and fasting needs to become an ever-increasing part of your life. Even the Pharisees fasted twice a week (Luke 18:12), yet many disciples of Christ have a hard time fasting at all. I challenge you to start a weekly fasting schedule. The time is now to get our flesh out of the way. Fasting disciplines our flesh and allows us to keep our flesh under control, for when the flesh is under control, the Spirit can reign. A fasting lifestyle is beneficial not only in effectively casting out demons, but also in ridding unbelief for all other spiritual gifts and works.

GIFTS SQUANDERED

"He also who had received the one talent came forward, saying, 'Master, I knew you to be a hard man, reaping where you did not sow, and gathering where you scattered no seed, so I was afraid, and I went and hid your talent in the ground. Here, you have what is yours."
(MATTHEW 24-25)

"For to everyone who has will more be given, and he will have an abundance. But from the one who has not, even what he has will be taken away. And cast the worthless servant into the outer darkness. In that place there will be weeping and gnashing of teeth." **(MATTHEW 25:29-30)**

I was afraid. I knew I had something—I could feel it in my hand. The gift was within me—it was about to come out, but I was afraid. I didn't know how. I didn't know when. I was afraid of beginning, so I never did.

This will be the testimony of many while standing in front of God. The biggest reason for the squandering of our gifts is fear. We are afraid for various reasons, and that fear keeps many of us from taking the first step. There is only one first step in everything. After I took the first step in Hatfield Square, 25-plus people were changed and my gifting was spent well. I continued to see the Father deposit many other gifts in my life to glorify His Kingdom. I intend to use the one opportunity this short life brings to both develop and exercise the gifting He has deposited within me. The timeframe for using our gifts is growing shorter every second. We spend hours upon hours on things of the world designed by the enemy to distract us.

We end up as soldiers of war sitting at home watching TV, while the biggest war of the world is about to escalate. We are squandering our gifts. We say we don't know how, but we fail to understand that the act itself teaches us. The book of Acts is a collection of acts, not step-by-step instructions on how to heal the sick or cast out demons. We need to follow their example and act.

We have grown so used to being spoonfed into the Kingdom that if we can't find a how-to video online, we never do it. This is an urgent call from God to you today: Do not squander the gifts deposited within you. Stop being afraid and die to yourself. We all too often lift the desires and voices of people for our life above that of God. A desire to serve God's Kingdom should trump all others. For, at the last trumpet, every voice and opinion except One will be silenced. Nothing else in life matters more than fulfilling God's calling in your life and using what He has given you to achieve it. God is calling you to such an intimate relationship with Him that it will shine you as a light to the nations—who will be amazed by your holiness, talents, and giftings.

There is no more time to waste, no more TV shows and video games to get addicted to, and no more of what we want. It's over. It's time for Him to manifest in your life. Understand that He loves you, is cheering you on, and will never leave you. Use the gifts He has offered you in boldness, never abandoning it for lesser things or burying it out of fear. It might be easy to go play a video game because it's easier than proclaiming the gospel at your marketplace, but if only you took the first step, your life would change.

A first step is all it takes, because in that step all the lies of fear of the enemy will come crumbling down and nothing will be able to stop you. Fear of the world is a lie—it does not exist outside our own minds. Fear of God is Truth; it is the essence of our being and the world around us. When He speaks, the earth and all in it will quake. When the world speaks, they utter mere words that can't touch eternity. But you can touch the eternity of the world, for God lives in you and chooses to speak through you if you step out of the way and let Him.

Many in the Truth Group are squandering their gifts. God has equipped them with a greater measure of Truth, yet they oppress the Truth by oppressing the Spirit. They never step outside the walls of the fellowship home, and the spiritual gifts never develop within the fellowship home, because they are afraid. You would be surprised at the incredible shift that stepping out for the first time makes in your life. Continue it into your fellowship, workplace, grocery store, etc., and you will soon walk just as He walked.

Sure, it will cost you your life—but who cares about this world anyway? We profess to follow Him, so why fear? What will you accomplish by allowing fear to overtake you? Walk in His power and let the blessing overtake you.

He that saith, I know him, and keepeth not his commandments, is a liar, and the truth is not in him. **(1 JOHN 2:4)**

You can study as much of the Torah as you want, but if you are not using your unique giftings (which are not limited to the official spiritual gifts) to glorify His Kingdom, you are missing the mark. It's not just about growing in knowledge—the Pharisees had that, but it was powerless, Spiritless, and ultimately null and void.

Do not miss this opportunity, as you will never get this chance again. I am speaking not only of this "test of life" we find ourselves in, but also the honour that comes with it—the honour of seeing someone healed by our hands; the honour of casting a demon out alongside Him; the honour of seeing someone tear up after they "clicked" the love of God; or the honour of seeing someone's mouth hang wide-open while hearing the gospel for the first time. Don't you understand? It will never again be possible! We are entering an age soon where all these things will no longer have application—for ALL will know, all will be healed, all will be fulfilled. But it's not here yet. Get out of your comfort zone. Die to yourself and follow Him.

It greatly distresses the Father that so many believe they "know Him," yet are passive for the Kingdom. Although they spend much time in His Truth, even in His presence, they never actually use what comes from it to save the world. They condemn the world as lost, and in their pride never go to love the world unto repentance. It is an attitude bred in fear, pride, and self-righteousness—enslaved by the enemy unto passivity and lukewarmness.

Yes, there are Torah-observant people who are lukewarm! God says that because you are not on fire, but rather lukewarm, He will spit you out of His mouth into a place of "gnashing of teeth." What if the "gnashing of teeth" occurs not merely because they are in physical pain, but because of regret? Their regret of squandering the gifts will haunt them unto eternity.

Imagine that. The trumpet blows. The time is up. You missed out. You know Him, but never used what He gave you. On Judgement Day, you are asked what you did with your giftings. Where is the increase? Where is the fruit? Where is the result of the Father's investment?

This is not a works-based gospel. We are not talking about working for His acceptance; we are talking about realising we are accepted and working from that identity. If you really believed what He said, you would understand that you are a royal priesthood ordained as a light of righteousness to the nations. If you never believed this—listened to it and obeyed (Shema)—then it is sin. We cannot expect to be received as a royal priesthood when we don't act like a priest, or don't even believe we are one. For if we truly believed, we would walk as one.

Again, the Hebrew mindset requires actions to follow our words. In that proclamation that we are a royal priesthood and part of Him, the royal priesthood needs to present themselves as a living sacrifice unto others. There is no greater love than this—for one to lay down His life, even for His enemies. If you don't lay down your life for His sake, you will not lay down your life for those He laid His life down for. The Father expects us to treat His and our enemies in that way—for no one will see God without love and holiness.

BLASPHEMY AGAINST
THE HOLY SPIRIT

Within both the Grace and Truth groups discussed in this book, the blasphemy of the Holy Spirit needs to be addressed. This important topic is not discussed nearly as much as it needs to be. This sin was described by Yeshua as the "unforgivable sin."

How ironic that the one sin Yeshua stresses as "unforgivable" is the very one we are uncertain of its meaning. As mentioned previously, the enemy changes definitions to cause disunity, confusion, and a lack of knowledge that leads to destruction. The statements Yeshua made around this sin are probably the most dire and fear-evoking when understood correctly. When I came to the revelation of this, it was not a happy moment for me. Memories started flooding through my mind of people whom I know might stand guilty of this sin.

Because it is so harsh and eternal, many have made excuses around or downplayed the words of Yeshua. This is a crafty work of the enemy to silence this important teaching of Yeshua, because Satan knows that if he cannot touch us directly, then he can get to us by denying the Holy Spirit.

The blasphemy against the Holy Spirit is the most extreme place to reach when the pendulum has swung way too far. It demonstrates the destruction of living outside the balancing unity of Spirit and Truth. Before reading this section, I ask you to take a moment in prayer before the Father, asking Him to guide you in the reading and discernment of this. The reason I state this is, considering the enemy's attacks on this teaching of Yeshua, it should not surprise us that Satan would try to use this teaching against us to separate us from God through his crafty lies. If he cannot make us ignore this teaching, as he has been doing, then he will try to lie about it.

To discern this correctly, we need to go to the encounter that led Yeshua to address the issue:

As the crowds follow Yeshua, eager to hear His words, a demon-possessed man appears. He looks the possessed man in the eyes and calls out, "You wicked spirit, be quiet! Come out of him!" The possessed, blind and deaf man is healed, being able to both speak and see.

The people quarrel amongst themselves. "Is this not the son of David, the Messiah the prophets spoke of?" As the Pharisees heard this, they were enraged with jealousy that the people would pay attention to such a man. They said amongst themselves that He casts out demons by Beelzebub, the prince of demons (Matthew 12:24).

Yeshua, having discerned their thoughts, said to them:

Every kingdom divided against itself is brought to desolation; and every city or house divided against itself shall not stand: And if Satan cast out Satan, he is divided against himself; how shall then his kingdom stand? But if I cast out devils by the Spirit of God, then the kingdom of God is come unto you. **(MATTHEW 12:25-28)**

Wherefore I say unto you, All manner of sin and blasphemy shall be forgiven unto men: but the blasphemy against the Holy Ghost **shall not be forgiven** unto men. And whosoever speaketh a word against the Son of man, it shall be forgiven him: but whosoever speaketh against the Holy Ghost, it **shall not be forgiven him**, neither in this world, neither in the world to come. **(MATTHEW 12:31-32, EMPHASIS ADDED)**

This is the teaching and context around the blasphemy against the Holy Spirit. It is a very specific situation, with a very specific accuser—the Pharisees. Yeshua said that Satan cannot cast out Satan, a very simple and logical teaching. There is light and darkness; there is no grey area in the spiritual realm. We don't have demons working in people to cast out other demons, but rather they work together to oppress or possess the individual. This is critical: Satan will never cast out Satan; a demon will never cast, or seem to cast out another demon, regardless of how we feel about the doctrine being taught by the man casting out demons.

Yeshua then states that He cast out devils by the Spirit of God—a sign that the "Kingdom has come upon them." He is teaching further that if it is not darkness that casts out darkness, it must be the light. We know that the Spirit of God is the set-apart Spirit of the light.

What He says next is critical. In relation to the accusations of the Pharisees, Yeshua teaches what blasphemy of the Spirit of God is—the sin the Pharisees committed, for which there is no forgiveness in this world or the world to come.

But what was the sin? Calling the clean, righteous, and pure Holy Spirit of God an unclean spirit—calling the Holy Spirit a demon. Yeshua ends the teaching by stating that "whoever is not for Me, is against me." (Matthew 12:30) It is by this we know that if we are in and for Him, we will never speak blasphemy against the Holy Spirit. If the Holy Spirit dwells in us, it is not possible for us to blaspheme against that Spirit, for the Holy Spirit does not blaspheme against Himself, just as demons do not cast out other demons.

They shall teach my people the difference between the holy and the common, and show them how to distinguish between the unclean and the clean. **(EZEKIEL 44:23)**

In other words, no matter who casts out a demon, by stating that it is a demon casting out a demon, we commit blasphemy. We are either in the Kingdom of Light fighting against the kingdom of darkness, or we are of the kingdom of darkness fighting the Kingdom of Light. There is no "gray area" or fence to sit on—in fact, the fence belongs to Satan.

Are you gathered together with Him, or are you a wolf who attempts to scatter His sheep like the demon attempted to do? If we stand in the way or oppose the casting out of demons, we are participating in the works of demons and we know Him not:

He that is not with me is against me; and he that gathereth not with me scattereth abroad. **(MATTHEW 12:30)**

It is important to understand the nature of the Pharisees whom Yeshua addressed. They did not understand the consequences of their actions, but their hearts were wicked and demonic. If we understood the severity and true consequences of our actions, we would probably not commit the sin. Blasphemy is not really a sin someone wants to commit, no matter their hearts. But committing this sin reveals the true nature of the heart. Those who commit this sin might be religious, but are not in true relationship with Yeshua. The Pharisees were condemned even before committing the sin: they had no relationship, no repentance, wicked hearts of deceit that perverted the Words of God into self-seeking and self-glorification. They've already mixed the holy and clean Word (Truth) of God with their added man-made teaching and traditions that nullify the Word of God (Mark 7:13). But their mixing of the Clean and Holy Spirit of God with the unclean wicked spirits of Satan was the end of the line.

In this I would like to stress that if you do not fit the profile of these Pharisees, but do have a real, intimate relationship with Yeshua, then it would not have been possible to commit this sin. This sin is not only in action, but also through the intentions of the heart. The Pharisees knew that Yeshua was doing good—preaching repentance, healing the sick, etc.—yet they still persecuted him as a devil. Their complete lack of understanding of the difference between good and evil, and the consequent evil direction of their hearts, led to this. This sin was not committed out of ignorance, but rather a conscious opposition to that which is good, pure, and kind—the Kingdom of Light.

To further understand, we see the disciples also making a similar mistake to the Pharisees, but with one important difference. When they persecuted a man casting out devils in the name of Yeshua and forbade him to continue, Yeshua told them to not forbid him, for he is in either the kingdom of darkness or the Kingdom of Light. We know that the casting out of demons is **always** a part of the Kingdom of Light.

And John answered him, saying, Master, we saw one casting out devils in thy name, and he followeth not us: and we forbad him, because he followeth not us. But Jesus said, **Forbid him not**: for there is no man which shall do a miracle in my name, that can lightly speak evil of me. For he that is not against us is on our part. **(MARK 9:38-41, EMPHASIS ADDED)**

The difference between the Pharisees and the disciples is that the disciples didn't call the Spirit a demon. Because the Spirit of God was upon the disciples, they had supernatural discernment. Even though they forbade him because they were intellectually unsure, they did not call the Holy Spirit unclean, or attribute the work of the Holy Spirit to a demon.

They were unsure of the teachings of the man that casted out the demon; in other words, they were unsure if the man was walking in the balance between Spirit and Truth. Did this man preach the fullness of Truth to go with the workings of the Spirit? This was their dilemma, not that he was doing so by another spirit.

The reality is that many who cast out demons and work other wonders by the Holy Spirit have terrible theology. While we should correct them and stand for the Truth, we should never call the work of the Holy Spirit in them the work of a demon. While Yeshua told His disciples that he is for them—that they should not forbid him—we also see the Father giving instructions around false prophets:

If there arise among you a prophet, or a dreamer of dreams, and giveth thee a sign or a wonder, And the sign or the wonder come to pass, whereof he spake unto thee, saying, Let us go after other gods, which thou hast not known, and let us serve them; Thou shalt not hearken unto the words of that prophet, or that dreamer of dreams: for the LORD your God proveth you, to know whether ye love the LORD your God with all your heart and with all your soul.
(DEUTERONOMY 13:1-3, EMPHASIS ADDED)

In the famous Deuteronomy 13 test, God states that there will be people doing signs, wonders, and even making prophecies that come to pass, but they will lead you away from the Truth to other gods or instructions of serving. The Father then says that He will allow this to happen in order to test us—whether we have built our houses on the rock.

Exercising discernment over spirits is so difficult at times that the Father has given followers a special gift of discernment. This gift is not always at work in every believer, but should be pursued, and for that reason I warn you: do not call out a spirit as demonic unless you are certain. I would like to submit that a time will come when God will test His people's foundations—where great signs and wonders will be done in His name, yet they will teach lawlessness and lead many away from His commandments. Could it be that these miracle workers, in some cases, are performing miracles by the Spirit of God? We know our own lawlessness does not stand in the way of the Spirit working through us; in that case, He would not be able to work through any of us! But I do believe sometimes God heals someone or casts out a demon by His Spirit through imperfect vessels—even vessels that do not proclaim the Truth—because He is a loving Father that wants to heal and set people free, and He can accomplish that even in the midst of lawlessness.

Of course, not every spirit or miracle is of the Holy Spirit. We will discuss the counterfeit Holy Spirit in the next chapter. But we can understand that God may allow this at times when we see what He tells many of these who will appear before His Throne:

Not every one that saith unto me, Lord, Lord, shall enter the kingdom of heaven; but he that doeth the will of my Father which is in heaven. Many will say to me in that day, Lord, Lord, have we not prophesied in thy name? and in thy name have **cast out devils?** and in thy name done many **wonderful works?** And then will I profess unto them, I never knew you: depart from me, ye that work **iniquity**.
(MATTHEW 7:21-23, EMPHASIS ADDED)

Because we have already established that a demon cannot cast out a demon, we can clearly see a group who call Him "Lord" that does many wonderful works, including the work of the Spirit of God that casts out demons. Yet in the end, He sends them out of His sight and says, "I never knew you." Therefore, while they were accomplishing mighty ministry works for God, they never knew Him and He never knew them—there was no true relationship. It is scary to think that these men were shocked at God's response, but God makes the reason very clear: iniquity.

If we state that we "know Him" and call Him "Lord," yet do not do what He says, we are liars and the Truth is not in us (1 John 2:4). We can convince ourselves we have relationship, but if we do no hear and obey (Shema), we deceive ourselves, and He will send us away.

The key word used in this passage to describe the nature of our deception is iniquity in the King James Version. Strongs G458 describes this Greek word—anomia—as illegality, a violation or transgression of the law. These people were doing works of the Spirit of God, yet were in violation, transgression, and rebellion against the law. They call the law of God abolished, unholy, or a "burden." It will cost them everything, and all the works they accomplished for the Kingdom of God will be as null and void in His sight.

Yeshua says that not one yot or tittle will pass from the Torah (law) until everything is over (Matthew 5:17).

Whosoever therefore shall break one of these **least** commandments, and shall teach men so, he shall be called the **least** in the kingdom of heaven: but whosoever shall **do** and teach them, the same shall be called **great** in the kingdom of heaven. For I say unto you, That except your righteousness shall exceed the righteousness of the scribes and Pharisees, ye shall in no case enter into the kingdom of heaven.
(MATTHEW 5:19-20, EMPHASIS ADDED)

Why is blasphemy against the Holy Spirit considered such an incredibly serious sin? The Holy Spirit is the witness and comforter sent by Yeshua to manifest the power and moving of God in this world. If we call Him a demon, we distort the very Image and Witness God has sent in this present age. Yeshua said, after casting out the demon,

"But if I cast out devils by the Spirit of God, then the kingdom of God is come unto you" (Matthew 12:28). By this we know the Holy Spirit was sent to manifest the very Kingdom of God. By distorting and opposing this, we directly oppose the works of goodness manifested by the Kingdom of God, and we cannot be from that Kingdom.

After the night at Hatfield Square, I wanted to tell everyone! But there was actually an astonishing amount of believing brothers and sisters who thought that praying for the sick was "weird," and it scared them, much in the same way the disciples were scared when they saw Yeshua on water before they received the Holy Spirit. The carnal mind is truly at enmity with these works, and we need to be careful not to judge a work by "what seems right to a man," but rather what is right considering scripture. Labelling true works of the Holy Spirit as demonic, like the Pharisees did, places us under risk of blasphemy of the Holy Spirit— an unforgivable sin very prevalent amongst those with an appearance of religion but without true relationship with their Creator.

THE KUNDALINI COUNTERFEIT

Only after understanding the blasphemy of the Holy Spirit can we really talk about the enemy's counterfeit; unless we understand the seriousness and discernment required to not blaspheme the Spirit of God, we are not ready to discern the counterfeit. If you have not read the previous section, "Blasphemy against the Holy Spirit," please read it before the following section.

While there are many mighty works that will be done by "men of God" through the Spirit of God—but who are operating in lawlessness—there is another danger: works done by men not of God, but by an entirely different spirit. This "other spirit" is also known as the Kundalini spirit, as classified by those in the Hindu/Occult/New Age movements. Kundalini means "serpent"—a demon that seeks to act under the persona of the Holy Spirit, even infiltrating churches, whilst working undercover for the kingdom of darkness.

Kundalini works undercover, but only in the sense of masquerading as an angel of light. While most demons hide inside the host and try their best to remain undiscovered, the Kundalini spirit is not as shy. We need to understand that this is planned and by design.

Why does this spirit act in this way? To pervert and cause confusion around the works of the true Holy Spirit. Most believers don't have the gift of discerning spirits, nor the biblical understanding of Truth to do so. We know only what we've heard in church, and most believers never truly get personal with God. Without a personal relationship, our discernment would be as good as those certain Pharisee's.

The inability of discerning spirits in both conventional Protestant and Charismatic circles has caused damage on both sides. Many Protestants believe it's mainly the Charismatic believers who are affected, but they fail to understand that they themselves are an even bigger target. But how?

Even though the Kundalini spirit seeks to oppress a host, the primary objective of the spirit is to destroy the reputation of Holy Spirit. Unfortunately, he has succeeded in many circles. The confusion created by this spirit has caused many conservative Christians to label any spiritual work that seems "a little weird" as demonic. It also has thrown the Truth Group into such fear of walking in the power of the Holy Spirit, because they don't know what is true or false anymore. Understand this: The biggest goal of the Kundalini is not demonic oppression, but creating a generation of passive believers too afraid to walk exactly as Yeshua walked—in great power of the Holy Spirit.

There are many cases where believers call, and will continue to call, the clean Holy Spirit an unclean Kundalini spirit; in doing so, they miss their calling of walking in the power of the Holy Spirit because they thought of it as evil.

DISCERNING THE SPIRIT

How do we discern what we are dealing with? First, it is very important to understand that you cannot discern through how you feel about a situation. If a true believer was to walk on water, most other believers would be as scared as the disciples, and a few Pharisees might even call it demonic. We forget that Yeshua walked on water and turned water into wine, and that He says that we will do the things He did—even greater things than these (John 14:12).

After the outpouring of Holy Spirit at Shavuot (Pentecost), and the manifestation of speaking in tongues, one of the first reactions of the people was to assume that those on whom the Holy Spirit fell were "drunk with wine" (Acts 2:13). We hear the same comments by many who witness speaking of tongues today. By this, we need to be careful not to pass judgement merely by appearance or how we feel.

As previously discussed, judging by your flesh or by what seems right is not the way to go. Scripture lays out a few key principles around discerning the spirit:

1. The Holy Spirit will always confess that Jesus is Lord

Now concerning spiritual gifts, brethren, I would not have you ignorant. Wherefore I give you to understand, that no man speaking by the Spirit of God calleth Jesus accursed: and that no man can say that Jesus is the Lord, but by the Holy Ghost. **(1 CORINTHIANS 12:1, 12:3)**

It is not possible for a false Holy Spirit to call Yeshua divine, blessed, or "Lord." It is spiritually impossible to give God any glory except by the Spirit of God. The kingdom of darkness is at enmity with the Kingdom of Light. When Yeshua asked His disciples, "Who do you say that I am?" (Matthew 16:16), Peter replied, "You are the Son of God!" Yeshua continued to say that this was not revealed to Peter by flesh or blood, but by the Father.

While it is only by the Holy Spirit that we can call Yeshua "Lord," demons can also acknowledge His identity (they can see it in the spiritual realm). When Yeshua cast out the demons, they screamed, "Truly! You are the Son of God!" (Luke 4:41), and they were right. But there is a difference between recognizing His identity and recognizing His divinity—Yeshua as Lord. If an army general were to meet the general of the opposition, he would address him by his title: General. However, that officer would probably not call the other "Sir" or acknowledge him as "Lord" unless he had already been conquered.

While the enemy is soon to be conquered once and for all, his kingdom has not been conquered yet. Until then, demons may believe and recognize the identity and even power of God, but they will never give Him glory or call Him "Lord." Therefore, it is important to note whether the spirit is merely recognizing His identity or also honoring His divinity.

Thou believest that there is one God; thou doest well: the devils also believe, and tremble. **(JAMES 2:19)**

When you pick fruit off a tree, you take a good look at it, analyse it, and judge whether it is fit for consumption. If you know what to look for, most fruits can be discerned in this way. However, in some cases, you realise the rottenness only when you open the fruit up.

In the same way, the Father instructs His children to "judge by the fruit." He gives us a list of both the fruit of the Holy Spirit and the fruit of the flesh:

But the fruit of the Spirit is love, joy, peace, patience, kindness, goodness, trustworthiness, gentleness, self-control. Against such there is no Torah. **(GALATIANS 5:19-21)**

And the works of the flesh are well-known, which are these: adultery, whoring, uncleanness, indecency, idolatry, drug sorcery, hatred, quarrels, jealousies, fits of rage, selfish ambitions, dissensions, factions, envy, murders, drunkenness, wild parties, and the like – of which I forewarn you, even as I also said before, that those who practise such as these shall not inherit the reign of Elohim. **(GALATIANS 5:22-23)**

So not only do we judge by the outer appearance of the fruit (what is on the outside), but we also look at the inner fruit—the intentions of the heart—and the ultimate outcome (results) of the manifestation. We do not judge on what the person who received the encounter decides to do with it, but rather what the fruit of the encounter itself is.

There is a difference between the two. I've seen a multitude of consequences after someone was healed. In two cases of people who receive radical instant healing, one will get on their knees and repent of their sins, while the other will rebel, and the seed sowed into them will fall on rocks and wither away. While the same Holy Spirit of God touched both individuals, the outcome is not the same. It is our job to manifest the love of God, but it is the responsibility of the individual on what he or she does with it. In this way, we cannot determine the spirit behind it based on what the encounter caused the person to decide, but rather what the encounter **encouraged** the person to decide. People have free will, and that free will choice often goes against the loving intention of Holy Spirit, especially within unbelievers.

Therefore, we need to look at the simple intention of the encounter. In the moment of the encounter, is the person experiencing a greater awe of God, leading to an encouragement of introspection and change? Whether repentance is taught alongside is irrelevant—for someone working in the Holy Spirit can have a lack of Truth in preaching repentance—but what is being encouraged by the encounter?

The Kundalini spirit encourages lawlessness; the Holy Spirit encourages obedience to the Torah (teaching) written on the heart. The Kundalini spirit manifests fruit of the flesh; the Holy Spirit manifests fruit of the Spirit. If the fruit is unclear in the moment, hold off on a judgement, enter intimacy with the Father through prayer and fasting, and then decide.

3.   A kingdom divided against itself cannot stand

Demons cannot cast out demons. It is not possible. No matter how "weird" the work of the spirit seems, if demons are being cast out, it is not done by a false holy spirit.

It is important to note that the fullness of Truth does not always accompany the work of the Spirit. Therefore, while we might be able to accurately discern the spirit behind the work, we also need a discernment of Truth to see if the truth that accompanies the work is trustworthy. For many will do mighty works in His name by His Spirit, yet hear the Father say, "Depart from me, you workers of lawlessness" (Matthew 7:23).

SPEAKING IN TONGUES

Before reading this section, please ensure you have first read the previous sections, "The Kundalini Counterfeit" and "Blasphemy Against the Holy Spirit."

Like a few other topics we've explored in this book, a lot of confusion surrounds the gift of speaking in tongues. Most of us are familiar with the charismatic outbreak of the gift that started in the mid-late 20th century. In some instances, the churches who practiced this gift also had other strange manifestations following them, such as barking like dogs, or even acting like snakes within the church. Some of these events are due to the invasion of the Kundalini spirit into many Christian churches, as discussed in a previous section ("The Kundalini Counterfeit").

Because this behaviour is in some cases associated with the same congregations that practice the gift of speaking in tongues, it has caused much confusion. I left this gift for last in this writing because we need to understand the nature of the Kundalini spirit before being able to discern this gift more accurately. I would like to remind you that the number one goal of the Kundalini spirit is to destroy the image of the true Holy Spirit by attempting to copy and distort His holy works.

I would like to submit that this has been Satan's assignment on this gift—mixing the holy gifts of God with profanity, disrupting its image and causing such confusion in the body of Messiah that nobody knows what is true anymore. This even leads many conservative churches to label everything connected to these Kundalini churches as demonic. Yes, these churches are causing much destruction in the lives of many by bringing in strange fire, but we need to remain vigilant around the goal of the enemy and not play ourselves into his hand by denying the Spirit when we intended to deny the counterfeit. Many of these churches also pray for healing—does that mean the gift of healing, properly exercised, is demonic? Of course not.

Apart from this, further confusion has arisen because of our carnality. As mentioned, our flesh is at enmity with God (Romans 8:7), and anything spiritual will offend our flesh. But because we do not walk by the flesh, but by the Spirit that confirms and follows the Word, let's put down our denominational lenses and look at this with a clean heart. I would also like to remind you that the first reaction men ever had towards the gift of speaking in tongues was to accuse the disciples of "being drunk with wine" (Acts 2:13). Let's not make ourselves guilty of the same sin through our lack of the discernment only the Spirit of God can bring.

My personal experience with the gift was like many others. Growing up in a Dutch Reformed church, and being totally disconnected from the charismatic movements, I had never heard or seen it. My first encounter with the gift was with a small gathering praying over one of my friends who had just accepted Yeshua as his Messiah. One of the people praying over him started praying in a language I had never heard before. As a young boy, unexposed to it, I felt quite uncomfortable.

Due to not being in such circles often, I never encountered this again—until a few years later when I read about it in the Book of Acts. Apart from the growing desire inside me to see healing, miracles, and other things Yeshua saw, this gift caught my attention. I started desiring it as the Father instructs us to (1 Corinthians 14:1), and I had a supernatural encounter a few months later.

On an ordinary night while on my knees in prayer, out of nowhere I heard the Spirit whisper, "It's time to speak now. You have it." In faith, I opened my mouth, and it was like rivers of living water started flowing from it. While I had full control over my actions, my mind was unfruitful in determining what I was saying—but the Spirit was directing my speech. Today I have had similar things happen when preaching, and I end up saying things I may not even have known or connected until I said it.

What was happening to me is hard to explain, but it was incredibly edifying to my spirit, and I ended up praying in tongues for an hour straight. I had no one to teach me how to pray in tongues, force me to, pray for me to receive the gift, or influence me in any other way to attempt speaking in tongues. This encounter happened by my innocent heart reading it in Scripture and desiring the gift for the sake of edification.

The first attack of the enemy after this was to try to convince me that it was not real, that I was making it up, or that it was demonic. He uses our carnal mind, which is at enmity with works of the Spirit, against us to make us doubt. In the coming months, when I had no idea what to pray anymore, I sometimes attempted to pray in tongues. While I didn't have the words to describe my prayers to the Father, when I prayed in tongues it was like the Holy Spirit was my intercessor (Romans 8:26).

Not long after I started practicing the gift, I had the dream of Israel discussed earlier, and a multitude of other gifting was poured out on me by His grace as I desired each. When we visited the demon-infested church months later and faced about 15-20 people with demons during their baptisms, I had no idea what to say to these demons to make them leave. My knowledge and maturity at that point let me down, but I knew one thing: the Holy Spirit can do the speaking for me.

When the person hit the water for baptism and came up, instantly a demon started manifesting. Some of the demons hissed like snakes, convulsing the person violently. I raised my voice in authority and started speaking to it in tongues. In Acts 2:3, we read how "tongues of fire" rested on each of the people. When I spoke in tongues to these demons, it was like my tongue was a fire to them. As soon as they heard it, they started screaming and becoming very afraid. No demon lasted more than a minute or two, and every single one left the man or woman being baptised.

It was surreal. And from that moment on, I never had doubt in the gift of speaking in tongues again. I truly started understanding why Satan is so afraid of God's people walking in this gift, why Paul encouraged us all to speak in tongues (1 Corinthians 14:5), and why the Father pressed this topic on my heart so strongly for placement in this book.

TYPES OF TONGUES

In Corinthians, Paul describes the different manifestations of this gift and provides us with much guidance around it. One of the theological confusions around the gift is how the gift manifests and looks like in action. The reality of the matter is, without walking out what we preach or teach on, we will never be able to fully understand it. If we don't shema—if we only hear but never obey—we will never learn the fullness. As discussed, the Holy Spirit teaches us the spiritual gifts through experience when we walk them out in faith.

If someone has never walked out a spiritual gift, their understanding of it will be too limited to qualify them as a good teacher on it. I am not saying they are disqualified from teaching, but that they would not be able to accurately teach on it as they would if they walked it out themselves. This goes for all of the spiritual gifts. Shema is a concept for hearing and obeying not only Torah, but also the Spirit.

We need to hear the Word, believe it for what it says regardless of what we see around us, and walk it out in faith to let the Spirit teach and guide us.

In his first letter to the Corinthians, Paul describes the nature of the gift to us:

For he who is speaking in a tongue does not speak to men but to Elohim, for no one understands, but in the Spirit he speaks secrets. But he who is prophesying speaks upbuilding and encouragement and comfort to men. He who is speaking in a tongue builds up himself, but he who is prophesying builds up the assembly. Now I wish you all spoke with tongues, but rather that you might prophesy, for he who is prophesying is greater than he who is speaking with tongues, unless he interprets, so that the assembly might receive upbuilding.
(1 CORINTHIANS 14:2-5 ISR)

From this, we deduct 3 main points:

- *He speaks secrets in the Spirit to God, and no one else understands*
- *He builds up himself*
- *An interpreter can be present in some cases for edifying an assembly, but is not required when the individual builds up himself*

Paul makes it very clear that, at least in this instance, speaking in tongues can be a personal gift between man and God, where nobody else understands the language for the purpose of edifying the man personally. However, on a corporate level, Paul requires an interpreter to be present (1 Corinthians 14:27), because if nobody understands the tongue, the assembly is not edified and it is fruitless for everyone besides the person speaking to God.

It is important to note that, in the first verse, Paul does not nullify the reality that a certain manifestation of the gift exists that is a personal conversation between an individual and God where nobody else understands. But he also encourages those who speak in a personal prayer language to seek the gift of interpretation for interpreting the language so that they may also use the gift in an assembly to build up other believers by translating the revelation of Spirit:

So also you, since you are ardent for spiritual gifts, seek to excel in the upbuilding of the assembly. Therefore, he who is speaking in a tongue, let him pray that he might interpret. For if I am praying in a tongue, my spirit is praying, but my understanding is without fruit. **(1 CORINTHIANS 14:12-14)**

He also states that our minds are unfruitful while praying in tongues. We don't understand what we are saying, and it might even sound strange to our carnal nature. What we hear when speaking in tongues is only the audible, physical manifestation of a spiritual gift. In the spiritual realm, there is always an activity that takes place when we exercise a spiritual gift. Sometimes the spiritual activity causes a manifestation in the physical realm. Therefore, the physical manifestations of the spiritual gifts are supernatural and often strange to our fallen mind.

So then tongues are for a sign, **not to those who believe but to unbelievers**, and prophesying is not for unbelievers but for those who believe. If then all the assembly comes together in one place, and all speak with tongues, and there come in those who are unlearned or **unbelievers, shall they not say that you are mad?**
(1 CORINTHIANS 14:22-23, EMPHASIS ADDED)

There seems to be a contradiction in Paul's writings. He first states that the gift of tongues is a sign for unbelievers. This is clear in the outpouring of the Holy Spirit in Acts 2, for many observed the miracle that all could understand the tongues in their own language, and it brought many to repentance. But Paul then continues to state that if there is an assembly and we speak in tongues, they will think we are out of our mind.

While it seems confusing, Paul is speaking to an audience that understands that there are two manifestations of the gift of tongues. One being an unknown, personal prayer language that requires the gift of interpretation when used in an assembly—this manifestation of the gift is not for unbelievers but the upbuilding of believers. The other manifestation of the gift is when the Holy Spirit does a miracle through the same gift to make unbelievers understand what is being said in their own language—this is the sign/miracle seen in Acts 2.

Many disagree on this, saying no personal prayer language exists, yet when questioned, they will state that they have never seen the gift of tongues acted out ever! If God told you that He has gifted you with the gift of tongues, how will you walk it out consistently? Will you wait for the day God opens your mouth without your consent, or will you go and walk it out yourself by opening your mouth and speaking in faith? As with all the gifts, if you do not shema—if you do not act in faith and physically walk it out—the gift will not manifest even if you have it.

Jacob was a missionary in a foreign land. He was frustrated that he required a translator to follow him around wherever he went. One day, he found himself ministering to a pagan. In his frustration of trying to communicate, he prayed for the pagan in his gift of tongues. This was only the personal prayer language he had prayed alone to God with.

By the end of the prayer, he found the pagan abnormally excited, as he had understood every word spoken by Jacob in his own language! God determines the physical result and manifestation of all the gifts, but it is our duty to walk it out.

None of the spiritual gifts has passed away—our flesh just doesn't like or expect how they manifest sometimes. While I understand this may be a more difficult topic for many to swallow, I encourage you to forget about the teachings of men around spiritual matters for a moment and seek the Father for the truth regarding this, as well as any other controversial matter within this book. I was not taught these spiritual giftings by any man; in fact, I was never in congregations that practiced it! I believe that in the same way that I sought the Truth at the Father's feet with clean intentions and He showed up, He will do the same for you and not give you a stone when you ask for Bread. He is a good Father that desires to restore the fullness of Yeshua's walk to us.

I thank my Elohim I speak with tongues more than you all
(1 CORINTHIANS 14:18 ISR)

3.

CONCLUSION

CHAPTER 3

Conclusion

THE JEALOUSY OF THE JEWS

"I am the 'Aleph' and the 'Taw', the Beginning and the End, the First and the Last." **(REVELATION 22:13 ISR)**

In the book of Revelation, Yeshua calls Himself the beginning and end. The Hebrew words for beginning and end are Aleph and Taw, respectively (Alpha and Omega in Greek). The original ancient Hebrew pictogram for "Taw" is a cross, and for "Aleph" a lamb.

Figure 2 "Taw"   Figure 1"Aleph"

(images: www.ancient-hebrew.org)

The connection is clear: the lamb (Aleph) on the cross (Taw). How magnificent! There is something even deeper to observe, however. The two sticks of the cross Yeshua was crucified on are significant of an end-times prophecy in Ezekiel that is manifesting right before our eyes.

The prophecy of Ezekiel 37 is well known but misunderstood. God calls Ezekiel to call the Spirit from the four winds to breathe on the dead bones. Ezekiel called the Spirit twice. The first time (Ezekiel 37:5) ,the bones come together, the flesh and sinews appear upon the bones, but the Spirit doesn't enter. This was where God brought His army and scattered bones (Israel) together from Egypt and gave them the Torah at Mount Sinai. At Mount Sinai (the first "mark"/sign of Shavuot), we see the first appearance of the Set-Apart Spirit and its rejection by Israel.

Israel's bones (foundation/Truth) had come together, but there was no Spirit within them.

Ezekiel prophesied again and called the Spirit into the flesh (Ezekiel 37:9). Around 1400 years later, the second mark of Shavuot (Pentecost) arrived and the Holy Spirit was poured upon all flesh.

> Then he said unto me, Son of man, these bones are the whole house of Israel: behold, they say, 'Our bones are dried, and our hope is lost: we are cut off for our parts.' **(EZEKIEL 37:11)**

Ezekiel identifies these bones as the House of Israel (northern 10 tribes). And indeed, because the House of Israel was divorced, they were scattered and their hope was lost. But through the Messiah, they were reunited with the Bridegroom and their regathering was started.

The Hebrew letter "Taw" (the pictogram that looks like a cross) means "mark," "sign," or "signature." The two sticks that make up the cross are the two marks of Shavuot (Spirit and Truth) that bear the signature of Yeshua. These two sticks—one representing Spirit and one representing Truth—are explored further in the rest of Ezekiel's prophecy:

> Moreover, thou son of man, take thee one stick, and write upon it, For **Judah**, and for the children of Israel his companions: then take another stick, and write upon it, For **Joseph**, the stick of **Ephraim**, and for all the **house of Israel** his companions: And join them one to another into one stick; and they shall become one in thine hand.
> **(EZEKIEL 37:16-17, EMPHASIS ADDED)**

The first stick bears the name of the House of Judah—the two tribes of the Southern Kingdom (previously discussed in the chapter, "The Covenant People"). These tribes have become the modern identity of who we know today as the Jewish people. Hence Yeshua was classified as a Jew, since He was from the tribe of Judah (Hebrews 7:14).

The second stick bears the name of the House of Israel (also known as the House of Ephraim or House of Joseph)—the 10 tribes of the Northern Kingdom who have been scattered into all the world and have lost their identity.

What we are seeing is the Father breathing His Spirit into the bones of the House of Israel (10 tribes) and their bones coming together (regathering). This prophetic event causes the two sticks to come together—the House of Israel, and all the gentiles grafted therein, coming together with the House of Judah (the Jews).

These two sticks Ezekiel speaks of make up the very cross Yeshua was crucified on! It is through His sacrifice and outpouring of His Spirit and Truth that these two houses come together. Without Yeshua, there may be two sticks, but they never come together unless the Spirit is breathed upon the House of Israel. This means that the bones of Israel need to come together, receive His Spirit, and provoke the Jews to jealousy!

"And speak to them, 'Thus said the Master יהוה, "See, I am taking the children of Yisra'ěl from among the nations, wherever they have gone, and shall **gather** them from all around, and I shall bring them into their land. And I shall make them **one nation** in the land, on the mountains of Yisra'ěl. And **one sovereign** shall be sovereign over them all, and let them no longer be two nations, and let them no longer be divided into two reigns." **(EZEKIEL 37:21-22 ISR, EMPHASIS ADDED)**

This depends on you. The Father is raising you into His foundation of Torah and filling you with His Breathing Spirit. What will you do with it? We were born for such a time as this. To manifest the fullness of Yeshua to all nations, and especially our brother Judah, who has been veiled from seeing the Messiah. For centuries they have rejected Him, usually not because of who He is, but because of who we say He is. Christianity may have manifested His Spirit in some form, but it has started to preach a Messiah that abolished the Torah—a Messiah that came to create a new religion that opposes much of what the Father has given us from the beginning. If this was the truly the case, according to the Father's Word itself, then he must be a false messiah.

Deuteronomy 13 states that anyone who teaches that the law is abolished is a false prophet. By the mindset of the Jewish people who know the Scriptures, a messiah who "does away" with the Torah must be a false messiah.

But what if this Jesus was the Messiah unto the Jew first? Yeshua. His Hebrew name means Salvation. What if this salvation did not abolish what was given by the Father in the beginning, but was rather the very Word itself given in the beginning? Yeshua never came to abolish the Word—thereby abolishing Himself. He came to fulfil the Word—to fill it up to its fullness of meaning. He came to show us how to walk it out perfectly, and He instructs all His disciples to walk as He walked.

This is how we provoke the jealousy of the Jews. Not by great signs and miracles without the Torah, nor by legalistic obedience to the law without the loving works of the Spirit to show for it, but by reigniting Spirit and Truth within ourselves. This is the living sacrifice He desires.

Paul knew this, and confirms it by his explanation of the veil that covers our Jewish brothers:

According as it is written, God hath given them the spirit of slumber, eyes that they should not see, and ears that they should not hear; unto this day. **(ROMANS 11:8)**

I say then, have they [the Jews] stumbled that they should fall? Let it not be! But by their fall deliverance has come to the nations, to provoke them [the Jews] to jealousy.
(ROMANS 11:11)

For I do not wish you to be ignorant of this secret, brothers, lest you should be wise in your own estimation, that hardening in part has come over Yisra'ĕl, until the **completeness of the nations** has come in. **(ROMANS 11:25, EMPHASIS ADDED)**

The "completeness of the nations" spoken of by Paul are God's people—all who are grafted into Israel—who needs to awake to the fullness of Spirit and Truth and walk just as Yeshua walked to provoke the Jews to jealousy. Yeshua is not coming back until this happens. The fullness of the remnant is a requirement for provoking Judah and ensuring Yeshua's return. The King is not leaving behind one son for another; He is coming back for both.

THE PRODIGAL SON

Yeshua's parable of the Prodigal Son is about this prophecy. In Luke 15:11-32, He tells the story of a lost son who went to dwell amongst the pigs; and when he realised his need for his Father, he returned home in shame. But when the Father saw the lost son coming home, he slaughtered a fattened calf to have a great feast for the son's return.

However, when the Father's other son heard of this, he was provoked to jealousy:

"And answering, he said to his father, 'See, these many years I have been serving you, and I have never transgressed a command of yours, but to me you have never given a young goat, so I could rejoice with my friends." **(LUKE 15:29)**

This son was obedient and held on to the commands (Torah) of the Father dearly; in fact, he guarded it with his life. But the lost, lawless son who returned came back with a broken and pure heart that desired the Father's love. The Father gave a young goat, Yeshua, our Passover lamb, as the sacrifice for the son's return. Through Yeshua and the restoration of Spirit and Truth He brings, the other brother is provoked to jealousy and convicted to change his hard heart.

Keeping the commands was what the elder son—Judah—was good at. The yearning heart of the lost son—Israel—was led back to the Father by the Spirit. When these two sons make peace, the one brother will grab hold of the other, seeking his ways:

Thus saith the LORD of hosts; In those days it shall come to pass, that ten men (house of Israel) shall take hold out of all languages of the nations, even shall take hold of the skirt [tzitzit] of him that is a Jew, saying, We will go with you: for we have heard that God is with you. **(ZECHARIAH 8:23)**

Judah will teach Israel the Torah, and Israel will demonstrate to Judah the Spirit. The two sticks will become one in His hand, and in His hand is Yeshua—the fullness of Spirit and Truth.

The tzitzit was given by God to Israel to wear as a remembrance of keeping His commandments (Deuteronomy 22:12). It is a symbol and witness of His commandments and set-apartness.

DECLARING THE LAST PREPARATION

And the dragon was wroth with the woman, and went to make war with the remnant of her seed, which keep the commandments of God, and have the testimony of Jesus Christ. **(REVELATION 12:17)**

In the end-time tribulation, Satan will go after the Spirit-Truth remnant—those who keep the commandments (Truth) of God and have the testimony (Spirit) of Yeshua. Satan is not particularly afraid of those who have one but lack the other, for only those walking in the fullness of Christ will destroy the works of the devil and possibly survive to see the end of the tribulation period.

TRUTH IN THE TRIBULATION: YESHUA'S MARRIAGE AND THE PROPHETIC CALENDAR

A spiritual shofar is sounding. A new awakening is occurring all across the world. One of the primary indicators of this awakening is God's people recognising the prophetic significance of His feast days. God has left us with a prophetic calendar to light our path in the uncertainty of these end-days.

Many consider God's festivals as "Jewish" because the Jews—our brother Judah—seem to be the only people keeping them. However, God states that these are in fact "My feasts":

Speak unto the children of Israel, and say unto them, Concerning the feasts of the LORD, which ye shall proclaim to be holy convocations, even these are my feasts. **(LEVITICUS 23:2)**

His feasts don't belong to anyone else, for He shares not His own glory.

Even more interesting, His festivals are all markers of His coming. The seven festivals of God are divided into four spring feasts and three fall feasts. The spring feasts have all been fulfilled to the very hour by the first coming of Yeshua; the fall feasts are left unfilfilled unto the hour of His second coming.

Yeshua was sacrificed as our passover lamb on the Feast of Passover, put in the grave on the Festival of Unleavened Bread, raised on the Festival of First Fruits, and 50 days later, the Holy Spirit was poured out on the Festival of Shavuot (Pentecost).

The timing is impeccable and was meticulously planned by the Father. This is why we often heard Yeshua say, "My time has not come yet" (John 7:6). As the true Messiah, He had to fulfil the Father's prophetic festivals to the very day. In regards to this, three fall festivals remain to be filfilled by Yeshua at His second coming.

There is a myriad of end-time voices sounding, but His voice trumps them all. The Feast of Trumpets is that voice. Just as prophesied in Revelation, the coming of the Lord Yeshua will be at the sound of a trumpet. The Day of Atonement (feast) is indicative of Judgement Day and teaches about the one and only atonement given by the Father. Lastly, the Festival of Tabernacles points to the coming wedding supper of the lamb, where the Bride of Christ will tabernacle with the Bridegroom.

Without studying and understanding these festivals, you cannot possibly understand or properly prepare for the second coming of the King. The timing and teachings around these festivals have been left for the Bride of the last days. The degree of revelation poured out around these in just the last eight years has been like never before in history. For the first time, those who have the Messiah are now starting to understand the fullness of His involvement in the festivals given in the Torah. The revelations of God will continue to increase as the birth-pains quicken.

The festivals are the wedding rehearsals left for the end-time Bride. You cannot enter a wedding ceremony without knowing the custom, having the correct garment, or without attending at the right time.

Yeshua's wedding parable was about this preparation! In Christianity, our divorce of the festivals of God has meant a divorce from preparation. It's time to start rehearsing for our wedding, for, whether we want to rehearse now or not, we will be rehearsing in the millennial reign of Christ:

And it shall come to pass, that every one that is left of all the nations which came against Jerusalem shall even go up from year to year to worship the King, the LORD of hosts, and to keep the feast of tabernacles. **(ZECHARIAH 14:16)**

Every year, Yeshua attends His wedding rehearsal, celebrates the Feast of Tabernacles, and seeks to meet His Bride there—even when she doesn't show. But the spiritual trumpet blast has started, and the Bride has started showing. Will you show up for that rehearsal to prepare for the coming wedding date?

Many say it's legalistic or "burdensome." Those who say it's legalistic to rehearse their wedding are not walking in love! While keeping His commandments can come from a heart of legalism, Love is not legalistic—and He seeks that love. I show up for a wedding not because I have to, but because I get to. I choose Him and He chooses me. I am my Beloved's and my Beloved is mine.

This book will not explore the endless depths of these festivals, but if you have never heard of this before, I encourage you to knock at His feet—the door will be opened to you.

In addition to the festivals, anyone in disobedience to the rest of His Torah (teaching), thereby walking in lawlessness (sin), will not be able to withstand the man of lawlessness to be revealed. If we do not build our house on the Rock—the Word that became flesh, the walking Torah—our house will fall by every wind of doctrine that will come forth from that lawless one. The anti-christ will perform many wonderful miracles, signs, and wonders—some even seemingly by the Spirit—and deceive, if possible, even the elect (Mark 13:22).

As mentioned in earlier chapters, keeping God's instructions also builds immense faith—a faith required to stand against the persecution of the world about to come up against God's royal priesthood. Things will get really hard. If you do not prepare now, it will be too late to build the necessary faith, and you will die in the wilderness. Most believers are not able to keep an instruction even as simple as the Sabbath now. How much more will they struggle with trusting the Father for enough manna on the six days to sustain them unto the seventh?

SPIRIT IN THE TRIBULATION: POWER AND FAITH REQUIRED IN THE GREAT TRIBULATION

Similarly, many who come to a deeper understanding of His truths have been left to mere physical observance, totally missing the spiritual depth and power. Keeping the Sabbath yet walking away from a blind man is powerless religion. The great tribulation will require us to walk not only in a state of holiness and obedience, but also in great faith and power.

Moses and the Israelites saw great wonders and miracles—the split of the sea (Exodus 14:21), the change of Moses' rod to a snake when confronting Pharaoh (Exodus 7:10), the facing of Nephilim giants (Numbers 13:33), and many other trials. The wilderness experience of the Exodus was a mere prototype and nothing compared to what will come. We face not only greater promises and miracles, but also greater trials. If we can't pray for a blind lady on the street due to what others might think of us, what makes us think we stand even a remote chance against the trials to come? You will not only need to die to yourself and the opinions of others, but also be willing to give up everything—even your children— for the call to come.

This fire of the Spirit is what enables this within you; it's not achieved by mere religious observance or behaviour modification. Take off your shoes, get on your face before Yahweh, and call on Him with the fast He desires (Isaiah 58:6) to make yourself more like Yeshua. This yearning needs to be so deep that you beg and knock until He gives it to you. God said He will allow us to see the things Yeshua did, and greater than these. Will we be the generation that for once actually believes these words? Or will we perish like our fathers in their unbelief?

The generations are coming to an end, and those around you need you to be the example of holiness and faith.

Where are those who enter homes to raise the dead, and who face the leaders and convict unto death? Where are the Spirit-men who call on His name, who fall by nothing and hold nothing in vain?

God calls you to pick up the cross of Spirit and Truth, to provoke both Jew and gentile to jealousy unto the fullness of Yeshua. If you squander your gifts for public approval, He will reject you on the great day of removal.

The increase of knowledge and Bibles in our hands leaves us with no more excuses. The time to prepare is now or never. Will you leave everything to follow what He believed, or hold on to what others believe about Him? I bring before you today a blessing and a curse: a blessing, if you follow what He has decreed from Genesis to Revelation and shema; a curse, if you do not heed this warning, but go on to lawlessness or passivity in faith, unprepared for the times to come.

My hope is that this book will encourage you and not distress you. There is still time, and while there is time, there is true grace. The Father has been patient, and while His patience is fading and the world is being prepared for great trials, He has not forsaken His Bride. We are truly witnessing the latter-day outpouring of His Spirit and Truth and the last great harvest. This outpouring, coupled with technology that brings an increase of information, will soon leave no one unreached by the true gospel, fulfilling all prophecies and paving the way for His return:

And this Good News of the reign shall be proclaimed in all the world as a witness to all the nations, and then the end shall come. **(MATTHEW 24:14)**

We are truly living in the most exciting season in all of history. Considering the Father's foreknowledge that we would be born for such a time as this, why do you think He has chosen us amongst other generations to witness this reveal? He has divine purpose and is trusting us with this.

Will we trust His capability of equipping us with everything we need to prepare? You cannot prepare alone, survive alone, or accomplish anything on your own. But with Him all things are possible, and He has given us the fullness of His power accessible by a simple prayer.

You were chosen for such a time as this because the Father adores you. You were not a mistake or a failure, but were ordained for the great purpose of facilitating His last great move upon the world. Do you not realise that we have been commissioned to change and impact the world in even greater ways than the first disciples did? What is to come will rival everything the world has ever known. But will you leave your world behind to follow Him?

PRAYER

Father, I come to you in repentance.

I have fallen short of your glory. In my lawlessness, I have trampled underfoot the Son of God. My lack of knowledge of your Truth has kept me from the fullness of Yeshua.

In my rejection of your Spirit, when I went by what seems right to a man, driven by my own carnal fears, I have kept myself from the fullness of Yeshua.

I give up. I surrender. For there is no other way. With men this is impossible, but by Your Name all things are possible. I thank you for freedom in my life, complete deliverance from every evil spirit that has lied to me or kept me back physically. I command complete healing over my body and mind right now. I thank you for renewing my spirit.

Yeshua, I call on Your name today for the fullness of Spirit and Truth in my life. Yahweh, I need this, for without You I have nothing of value to say or offer this fallen world. I love you, Yeshua. Prepare me for the wedding date.

Give me discernment in these times. Help me to be slow to speak, but make my cup overflow with the wisdom of your Spirit.

I pray this in the name of Yeshua, the Messiah. Amen.

LAST WORDS

My prayer is that the Father would use this book as a tool to ignite a fire of Spirit & Truth across the world. If this book has blessed you, please share it freely with your friends. May all who has an ear – hear.

For more teaching on the contents of this book, visit:
www.RiseOnFire.com

This book is available in both e-book and paperback on:
www.SpiritTruthBook.com

Made in the USA
Coppell, TX
21 March 2024

30264510R50089